Love of Mother Universe

Love *of* Mother Universe

Hua-Ching Ni and Maoshing Ni, Ph.D.

TAO OF
WELLNESS
PRESS

Los Angeles

The authors wish to express their appreciation to all students and friends who devoted their time and efforts to transcribing, editing, proofreading, typesetting and designing of this book. Publication of this work was made possible by an anonymous donor.

Published by:
Tao of Wellness Press (An imprint of SevenStar Communications)
13315 Washington Blvd., Suite 200
Los Angeles, CA 90066

Calligraphy by Maoshing Ni, Ph.D.

Library of Congress Control Number: 2008930407

Library of Congress Cataloging-In-Publication Data

Ni, Hua Ching.
Love of mother universe / Hua-Ching Ni and Maoshing Ni.—1st ed.
—Los Angeles : Tao of Wellness Press, c2008.

     p. ; cm.

     ISBN: 978-1-887575-26-3
     Includes index.

  1. Harmony (Philosophy). 2. Spiritual life. 3. Spiritual life—
Taoism. 4. Conduct of life. I. Ni, Maoshing. II. Title.

BL105.H37 N55 2008   2008930407
299/.514448—dc22   0809

*This book is dedicated to those who accept the
truth that all people are children of Mother Nature.*

*May this book help all of you wash away your painted faces
so that you can embrace each other with the one, deep love
from the heart of the Mother Universe.*

To All Readers,

According to the teaching of the Universal Integral Way, or Heavenly Heart, male and female are equally important in the natural sphere. This fact can be observed and confirmed in the diagram of the T'ai Chi. Therefore discrimination is not practiced in our tradition. All work is dedicated to both genders of the human race.

Wherever possible, sentence constructions using masculine pronouns to represent both sexes are avoided. Where they do occur, we ask your tolerance and spiritual understanding. We hope that you will take the essence of these teachings and overlook the limitations of a language in which gender discrimination is inherent. Ancient Chinese pronouns do not differentiate gender. We hope that all of you will achieve yourselves well above the level of language and gender. Thank you.

Warning—Disclaimer

This book is intended to present beneficial information and techniques that have been used throughout Asia for many centuries. This information and any practices that appear in this work utilize a natural system within the body; however, no claims are made regarding their effectiveness. The information offered is according to the authors' best knowledge and experience, and is to be used by the reader at his or her own discretion and liability.

People's lives have different conditions and their growth has different stages. Because the development of all people cannot be unified, there is no single practice that can be universally applied to everyone. It must be through the discernment of the reader that practices are selected. The adoption and application of the material offered in this book must, therefore, be the reader's own responsibility.

The authors and publisher of this book are not responsible in any manner for any harm that may occur through following the instructions in this book.

ABOUT THE AUTHORS

Hua-Ching Ni, author, teacher and healer, addresses the essential nature of human life and works to further the personal growth and spiritual development of this and future generations. He was raised in a family tradition of healing and spirituality that is being continued by his two sons, Drs. Daoshing and Maoshing Ni, and by his many friends and supporters throughout the world.

Dr. Maoshing Ni, D.O.M., L.Ac., Ph.D., Dipl. C.H., Dipl. ABAAHP, has lectured and taught workshops throughout the country on such diverse subjects as longevity, preventive medicine, Chinese nutrition, herbal medicine, acupuncture, facial diagnosis, *feng shui*, stress management, *I Ching*, meditation, *t'ai chi, chi kung*, and the history of medicine.

Dr. Mao has also authored many books, audio/video tapes and DVDs. These include *Chinese Herbology Made Easy, The Tao of Nutrition, The Eight Treasures Energy Enhancement Exercises, Self-Healing Chi Kung, 18-Step Harmony Style T'ai Chi, T'ai Chi Sword, Meditation for Stress Release, Pain Management, The Yellow Emperor's Classic of Medicine, Secrets of Longevity*, and *Secrets of Self-Healing*. He was also an editorial member for the best-selling book, *Alternative Medicine: The Definitive Guide*.

TABLE OF CONTENTS

PART VI   *Inspirational Readings*

大 愛 教 義

The Declaration of Universal Love
The Religion of the Yellow Emperor

The Yellow Emperor of ancient China, who reigned during the third millennium BCE, was one of humanity's great ancestors. He helped to develop the early humanistic culture known as the Way (or "Integral Way" as known today,) which embraces universal nature in personal and social life. He led people out of a primitive style of living into a civilized way of life whereby people pursued health and natural wisdom in all aspects of their lives. While other human races began worshipping a mentally-created image of God, he inspired people to be self-reliant and to respect and develop their innate spiritual vitality.

As emperor, he was considered the son of Heaven whose duty it was to treat and guide all people equally and impartially, just as the sky does. In fact, his name—the Yellow Emperor—hints at the sun whose light and warmth shines equally on all. Therefore, it follows that the Way, or universal religion of the Yellow Emperor, accepts all religious and spiritual groups that can work together to fulfill impartial Universal Love. Any individual and any social or spiritual group are welcome to accept and adopt the universal spiritual education of the Way, in order to help people understand and embrace the one family of humanity.

人類精神須更新,
捨狹隘而趨廣大.
棄私偏而從大公.
人之品位在大愛.
神之尊貴在大愛.

Our human spirit needs renovation
   in order to forsake its narrowness and become broad,
      and in order to give up its partiality and embrace universality.
The real spiritual value of a human life is Universal Love.
With Universal Love, God is given the highest respect.

發揮人性愛.
救世無良方,
大愛以爲教.

Developing universal humanistic love
 is the only remedy for a troubled world.
Universal Love is the new spiritual practice
 and new religion for the salvation of everyone.
Universal Love is the Way.

大愛不亂,
大愛不怯.
大愛不懼.

With Universal Love there should be no more spiritual confusion.
With Universal Love there should be no more cowardice.
With Universal Love there should be no more fear towards anyone or anything.

大愛不害.
大愛無毒.
大愛不求酬.
大愛不求報.

With Universal Love no harm is created.
With Universal Love no poison is brewed among people.
With Universal Love no rewards or favors are required.
Universal Love only asks for your acceptance and support.

以大愛改造人心.
以大愛拯救天下.
大愛必從小愛始.

大愛方得實踐.
有私愛不忽大愛.
因私愛推愛天下.

Universal Love can reform the minds of humanity and rescue the world.
The great love of humanity begins from personally loving yourself and your family.
By loving your own life and the life of your family,
    the great humanistic love of Universal Love can be fulfilled.
You should not indulge in small personal love and ignore the great love of humanity.
Rather, develop your personal love to embrace and envelop the entire world.

愛之毋立己,
立己愛不眞.
人能無私欲,
大可包天地.

Loving the world is not about establishing yourself.
If you have that intention your love cannot be true.
Only when you are able to manage your personal desire and ego
    can you embrace the entire cosmos.

天地爲心,
別無私見.
不重口號,
但重實踐.

Make Heaven and Earth your heart.
Give up your narrow-mindedness and your insistence on personal opinions,
    and value and love all of humanity as one life.
Slogans are not important.
The greatest value in life is realizing Universal Love.

INTRODUCTION

Our Direct Connection
with the Mother Universe

Just as friends can influence one another,
   the books you read can influence you as well.
Befriend those people and books that live not for just a single generation,
   but for the truth of life that spans all generations.
Then befriend the ageless truth of a healthy life of well-being
   in which there is Heaven on Earth and Heaven throughout the universe.
Offer your warm friendship to the mountains, seas, lakes and forests,
   for they all contribute to your well-being.
Take a sincere interest in the well-being of the world
   as an integral part of your individual life.
For wherever you go, whether to the bottom of the ocean or to a faraway star,
   it is only for a while—this world is where you live.
Throughout the last three to four thousand years,
   humankind has experienced many new things,
   but it is the age-old worship of the Mother Universe
   that continuously supports human growth and refinement.
In this book, I represent these things to you
   from my life experiences as I have journeyed through this world.

When we are children, we only know our Mother.
You may laugh at my efforts to offer you a treasure that you already have,
   but you might otherwise be tempted to throw away the old faith
   from which all new faiths were born.
You are drawn to the offspring, but not to the Mother,
   for she cannot make you rich or powerful,
   or help you wage successful wars over ideological beliefs.

I hope that I have done enough spiritual detoxifying work
   to enable you to see the direct relationship between you
   and the Mother Universe.
She is still the main partner of your life,
   just as she is with humanity itself.

I have not tried to remove the piles of colored stones
    that religious concepts have placed on your path to infinity,
    but I hope that my books will turn them into stepping stones
    that will help you cross the swift currents of life.

Who do you allow to block the truth of life from your children's view?
Do you pay nannies to put your babies to sleep by reading storybooks to them?
Do you pay a church or government to do the same for you?
I have condensed the bulk of the religious stories into a small, hexagonal diamond
    that is a world treasure on the shore of the ocean of life.
Getting lost in stories night after night,
    one might otherwise overlook Mother Nature
    who owns all the diamonds,
    including the diamond of your life.

Nature is alive; so are we.
Nature is complete.
The concepts and descriptions in books are not complete.
A description is not the real thing
    any more than a person's name is the real person.
The nature of the universe is too big to talk to the small life form of humans directly,
    but she is spiritually responsive through the invisible web of life.
That is how we can receive messages of enlightenment from Mother Nature,
    if we seek them.

There is no middle-man between you and Mother Nature.
You do not need an internet service provider to contact her.
Nor can any religious picture represent her being.
In fact, such pictures will only block your view of her.
Any view of Nature that is partial can be dangerous.
The Integral Way recognizes that human life
    is only a tiny part of the big life of the Mother Universe.

You can tell the Mother Universe all the troubles you have suffered
    that were caused by other people or by yourself.
Your persistent prayers will reach her.

She takes care of you and helps you grow,
    just as an earthly mother watches over and helps the growth of her children.
The Mother Universe is a safe haven for all of your emotions.
Her healing powers are the greatest doctor there is.

This book will introduce the Mother Universe to your mind and spirit.
Although the prayers contained here can connect
    your mind and spirit with the Mother Universe directly,
    there are many other ways to connect with her.
You can walk quietly in the forests and on the mountains,
    or by the lakes and seas.
Simply being close to the life energy of Mother Nature is a form of prayer
    in which you give Mother Nature the opportunity to care for you.
Although you can find emotional escape by
    sitting in front of the television or by going to the movies,
    these things cannot refresh you as Mother Nature can.
She refreshes you mentally, emotionally, physically, and spiritually.

Befriend the ageless mountains, lakes, seas, and forests.
Mother Nature stores invisible treasures there that will support your well-being.
Offer these gifts of Mother Nature your warm friendship directly—no e-mail, please.

Wherever people are crowded together,
    there will be mixed and confused energy.
Out in the open, where Nature is able to cleanse herself,
    you have a better chance to be refreshed and recharged.
There, the brotherly mountains, sisterly lakes, motherly oceans, and fatherly skies
    will take better care of you than you can yourself.
You can help by choosing the right exercises and spiritual practices,
    by behaving decently and wisely,
    and by following the principle of balance in the arrangements of your life.

PART I

A Bright World Begins with Observing Your Mind

Natural help comes to those with self-managed, serene minds.
Those who are busy-minded keep themselves away from the Truth of life.

Chapter 1

For What Would We Like to Prepare?

All of us receive both positive and negative conditioning from our families, culture and society. As adults, we are exposed to multitudes of information and ideas from religions, politics, educational institutions, the media and advertising, all of which try to win our favor. As children growing up with cartoons, computer games, school, friends, and parents, do you think we are safe living with the conditions that we or our caregivers choose for us? To put it simply, the healthy state of our lives is constantly being challenged by worldly life. It has become necessary to purify our bodies, minds, and souls daily, or at least weekly, by reexamining the influences with which we come into contact.

There may be a few individuals, families, and societies that are fortunate enough not to be affected by the surrounding negativity. There are also those who, through their own efforts, become aware of their conditioning and manage to reform their minds, and regain perfect health, or purity, and a natural life. The word "purity," to me, means a state of unaffected or benign health, and the word "natural," in its plain sense, means a state unaffected by artificial organizations or establishments. Unfortunately, such states have become luxuries in this stage of worldly life.

Ask yourself, what is the condition of my life now? Physically, mentally, and spiritually you are like an isolated soldier besieged by invisible enemies approaching from all directions. Being neutral and naive can be your best psychological safeguards. Also ask yourself, how much do I really need to know? It is worthwhile knowing useful things about the nature of your mind and spirit, and how to attend to their well-being, particularly when they are exposed to all sorts of conditions.

Although you have probably noticed that people can be negatively conditioned by politics, have you noticed that people can be negatively conditioned by religions? This situation is a little more subtle, since once a religion has become the social custom, you may not necessarily notice its negative effect. But overly religious people lose their common-sense understanding of natural life.

Life cannot only be defined by the life you experience today, particularly when you consider that your mind has been conditioned by all sorts of things. You should also consider what it was like before your life was formed. Was there any race or skin color? Did nationality exist? What passport did one hold? Before life existed, with what was there to identify? Reflecting on these questions may open you to experience your life as an earthling. All earthlings are related to the solar system. And to what is the solar system related? You may come to understand that life is the child of the Mother Universe, and that the identity you have insisted on and emotionally struggled for is a very limited view of life. In reality, earthlings are part of one big family that constitutes the universe.

No matter how different we are, we are all basically products of Nature, and as such, share the same root of life. Because we are a part of the universal nature, there is hope for anyone who can learn how to subject his or her personal desires and interests to universal conscience—the universal constructive nature—which is the true God of all lives. Unfortunately, most people limit their lives to the physical and/or mental levels where they fight for and die over small beliefs. But isn't life so much broader than small beliefs? Realizing the spiritual reality of the universe is the new frontier for human knowledge. It is, in fact, the process of the spiritual development of humanity. It is a task akin to instilling a conscience in a robot.

True help comes through spiritual education about the plain and natural truth of life. This is why Maoshing and I have begun to place more emphasis on Tao as the Way of the Mother Universe. We spread the message of confidence in the universal supportiveness of life, rather than in any small belief or psychological program. The emphasis on a new spiritual direction is a matter of offering a healthy spiritual education to help you understand what your problems are, and to appreciate what your true, broad nature is. Understanding will help you reduce conflicts and achieve peace and harmony. As your understanding deepens, you will discover that God is the universal subtle nature, not some narrow conceptual tool for psychological warfare or social power.

Spiritually, external hostility is the reflection of our own internal shortcomings. The real culprit is inside us. Narrow-mindedness is the real folly of life and the common enemy of humanity. For that reason, we should immediately mount an internal holy war against our own shortcomings, and transform them before they swallow us whole.

Spiritually developed individuals do not insist on their views, nor do they allow themselves to be disturbed by worrisome emotions or artificial worldly or religious ideas. By consistently keeping their consciousness clean from limiting concepts and negative interferences, they safeguard their health and nurture their spiritual nature.

When the worrisome and calculating work of the mind ends, the deep and subtle power of the Mother Universe can perform unimpeded in the spaciousness created by our naturally endowed optimistic nature. Our constructive spiritual nature can then fulfill our human life in the same way that the universal constructive nature fulfills the physical universe. Our relationship to the true reality becomes as simple as a fish enjoying its inseparable connection to water.

The cultural effect of the world's confusion is deep. Whose responsibility is it to fix the negative trend and safeguard the world? We hope each of you becomes aware of the call. What standard are you going to use to fix the unhealthy condition of the world? We humbly suggest that you refresh your mind, and spiritually cultivate yourself in order to free yourself from unhealthy and limiting conditioning. You will then be able to recognize that a universal and common sense standard of natural health and wellness is above conventional notions of society, religious notions of holiness, and meaningless sacrifice.

Chapter 2

The Common Disadvantage of the Mind

When we erect powerful spiritual images and insist on narrow beliefs, we limit our spiritual potential. Therefore, part of learning how to connect ourselves with the universal spiritual nature involves understanding the mind, and learning how to discipline it. We can then manage our emotions and free ourselves from psychological traps. The following discussion can help in this endeavor.

The mind pervades our entire being. One level of the mind is the emotions, which are reactions of the mind to internal and external information. Emotions can be healthy provided we do not indulge in them. When we are indulgent and demanding, mistakes and harm are caused. For example, greed can motivate you to achieve a better life, but once the fondness for something or someone persists, it becomes madness.

Greed, hatred, and passion are the three emotions most harmful to life. An overly passionate person is like a demanding or insistent person. When passion and insistence fuel other emotions, it can destroy the normalcy of life. Most of the physical conflict and suffering in the world is a result of mental narrowness and mental insistence.

Conventionally, spiritual leaders have used big and high ideas to offset the strength of passion in life, and thus various beliefs in God have been invented. However, those ideas have led to unreasonable faiths, wherein the very emotion spiritual leaders have tried to offset has caused people to insist on their beliefs to the detriment of other lives.

Using passion to support emotional insistence is the worst kind of action. It will inflate a problem to a point beyond help. The big events in history, such as the communist revolution in China, are the result of such misguided mental activity.

In order to understand our personalities and reduce our self-created obstacles, we need to recognize and appreciate our inner forces more deeply. Understanding will help us to manage and purify our lives, especially our minds, as well as help us to understand others.

Regular purification is needed in almost every stage of life because of the direct influence our mind has on our physical and spiritual growth. We should never wait for a situation to escalate to unhealthy levels. We can also purify our minds by purifying our soul.

The Various Levels and Functions of Our Internal World

Level One: The Sensory Organs and Their Functions

The sensory organs collect external information. There are seven levels, which are also known as the seven "generals" or deities. They are:

the nose for smelling;

the tongue for tasting;

the eyes for seeing;

the skin for tactile feeling;

the ears for hearing;

the combination of several senses or all of the senses functioning together to satisfy the preliminary inquiries of life; and

the spontaneous feeling about the general condition of the internal and external environment that produces an instant mental reaction to either like, dislike or ignore.

Level Two: The Emotions

Emotions can either produce clean fuel or energy for life, or a poisonous boiling force that spoils one's life and creates an unhealthy atmosphere. The degree of harm depends on the type of emotional reaction. Emotions such as fear, worry, anxiety, jealousy, depression, over-excitement, and fervor are unhealthy, while peace, pleasantness, and gladness are neutral emotions.

Most of us know that the content of our consciousness supports and decides the true being of what we are. However, we may not have noticed that our positive, clear thoughts can be affected by our moods and emotions. In addition, our different moods and emotions can also produce thoughts.

Indulging in moods such as irrationality, melancholy, despair, and irritability can lead to self-pity, depression, and psychological problems. Naturally, if we wish to cultivate an effective mind, we should not develop the habit of being emotional and moody. Nor should we base our decisions on those levels if we wish to avoid making significant and sometimes fatal mistakes. The mind of an emotionally indulgent person has lost its balance, and poor balance cannot support effective decision-making or constructively guide one's life.

The secret to a life of positive internal support is that a consistently peaceful and pleasant emotional state produces spiritual vitality, which works to further support our health and happiness.

Level Three: Individual Intelligence

The mental capacity of intelligence is the main headquarters of our life. It has four functions or generals which are:

the intellectual ability acquired through birth;

the intellectual knowledge acquired from institutional education and/or self-training;

the individual mental tendency or destiny; and

rationality or self-poise.

Level Four: The Conscience and Moral Sense

The conscience is the high adviser of one's life. It moves us to consider and respect our own lives and the lives of others, equally.

Level Five: The Divine Sense of Self-Surpassing

This sense inclines us to go beyond self-concern for a moral cause. It is the God within the depths of our life.

Level Six: The Soul of Life

The soul is the silent, subtle partner and provider of our life. Normally, she is unnoticeable. She is in the depths of our life, but she is not separate from our physical body. It follows that with a healthy and practical life, we can support the health of our soul. The soul, in turn, supports our longevity and life's performance. By protecting and maintaining our spiritual potency—the root of our life—we are given the opportunity to germinate our life in a different way.

Level Seven: The Direct Knowledge System of the Mind

There are five kinds of direct knowledge. They are:

the intuition that comes through a subtle and specific inner vision without any particular contact with people or things;

the intuition that enables us to know what has happened in a remote place or in a past or future time;

the ability of the spiritual mind to see and hear subtle messages about events which are unrelated or unconnected to our own life;

the natural self-healing system; and

the general sense of a life star which secretly guides our life.

(In truth, the general sense of a life star which secretly guides our life is a group of inner subtle energies which determine the quantity of happiness, misery, good fortune, and misfortune in our life. This group also determines our ability to develop beyond our current life conditions.)

All five types of direct knowledge determine the spiritual strength and power of our life. In some natural conditions, they operate as the spiritually functioning mind, which needs no support from the senses and physical organs. These functions collect the true and deep knowledge of life. However, their acceptance and effectiveness still depends on the management of the acquired conceptual mind (also known as the general or post-Heaven mind), since that mind, out of habit, controls our life. In contrast, the natural, universal or pre-Heaven mind, which is free of limiting conditioning, is not divided between itself and the spiritual levels of the mind. So cooperation between it and the spiritual level is much easier.

A great or high mind is a universal mind that has merged with the deep spiritual nature of life. The high mind is no longer under the distorted influence of personal thought and ambition, and so it reflects the constructive spirit of life purely. Because it is no longer obstructed by small, personal, and worldly concerns, it can see through all conceptual, psychological, and spiritual obscurities.

Only those who respect the subtle internal order of life can effectively set the external order of life. Order setting should not be dominated by the acquired or post-Heaven mind; it should follow the natural order of life, whereby the soul is respected as the lord or lady of life.

The soul is the true God in life. It is spiritually benign and neutral to the universal spiritual qualities of life. Because religious teaching can contaminate the soul's benign nature, it is the duty of a healthy individual to continually cleanse his or her mind and soul from limiting religious concepts and customs, and from limiting conditioning in general.

Life is the result of the convergence of all the different strengths of the aforementioned levels, and it is the soul that integrates and glues them together as one big unit. In its natural state, the soul is attuned to the Universal Way of life, which stands for the harmony and cooperation between all spheres of life. What generally happens, however, is that the conditioned mind (being a later development from the post-Heaven stage of life) usurps the soul's position, and takes charge of life. By taking control, the general mind exceeds its true function of being a servant of the soul.

The teaching of the Integral Way restores the original position of the pure mind (pure heart) to be above the general mind as it only represents a small portion of the heart. The general mind reacts to situations. It is flattered by intelligence, cleverness, and smartness. As it reacts quickly to changing circumstances, it lacks steadiness. The pure heart is different. It works honestly with the inner life and ignores the externals; thus it is steadier and more stable. Its shortcoming is that it tends to be less flexible in the performance of life.

Part of the duty of the teachings of the Way is to help you to positively educate your mind and manage your emotions. This guides you to develop the necessary mental and emotional maturity to appreciate the subtle levels and soul of your being, and to support a constructive and spiritually evolving life. You can then help others to do the same.

If you wish to nurture your life with the Way, the balance of the pure heart and the general mind is emphasized. If we look at the above levels, the senses serve the general mind and the heart neutrally and equally. The emotions, being closer to the physical nature, can cause sickness and obstruct the subtle performance of the heart. In Level Three, the first three functions are related to the intellectual level of the mind, while only the fourth function—rationality—looks for balance with the heart. Levels Four, Five, and Seven are the spiritual functions of our life, and Level Six is neutral as the soul or holder of life.

Spiritually, the Integral Way teaches about the soul or universal heart of life. Externally, it sets the focus on the universal high principles of Nature, and how they apply to life and society. The teachings are beyond the subjective dual sense of good or bad, and are beyond the personal views of individuals, families, friends, and groups. Subjective standards and artificial establishments only confuse the world. For example, some people define an individual according to how patriotic they are, or how religiously devoted they are. But, while that individual may be helpful to their nation or their religion, they can be hostile to other nations and other religions.

Whether a standard is universal or not is based on whether it leads to a natural and normal performance of life, or to a sub-normal performance. The word "normal" to me means a state of benign health unaffected by artificial organizations or establishments. In an individual, it is a state of health and balance that reflects the wider health and balance of the universal nature. Sub-normal refers to a temporary unbalanced state whereby an individual or society has gone against the natural flow and pattern of the universal nature.

The universal standard comes from a deep objective and intuitive perception of Nature, people, and their social groups. The setting of the universal standard is related to the rational force in life. In life, we need to search for the power of balance. If we were to reorganize ourselves constructively, the conventional religious sense of God and the impulse of life would withdraw to the background as the support for our life, while the emotion of life, which has become the prime preacher to the god of "I," would relinquish its insistence and become a simple interpreter of life's events. All important decision-making would become the duty of the new God of rationality, which would work together with the spiritual functioning of our being. Although still a part of the mind, rationality should become the top performer of the mind.

A developed mind is a reflective mind. The reflective mind connects to the deep, pure mind, or the spiritually functioning sphere of our life. Throughout the prehistorical stage of human life, all human progress and development was made through the power of deep perception and reflection. Many important perceptions about life were eventually recorded in the *I Ching: The Book of Changes and the Unchanging Truth (I Ching)*.[1] This work contains deep knowledge about Nature and life, as well as guidance to help you live naturally and peaceably. Consulting the *I Ching* as a way to study your life and the natural pattern behind human activities has spiritual value, while using it for mere fortune-telling does not. When our rational mind is still young, we are encouraged to consult with wise advisers before making decisions, and the *I Ching* is one such advisor.

If you learn the universal standard, you will know what is appropriate in a situation even before any consultation or divination. The simple guidance can be this: if circumstances and events are proceeding normally, it is good; if the result is doubtful, and especially if the result may cause harm, it is bad. You are also guided to know that it is unnecessary to establish ideas of independence, equality, and freedom based on pride. Spiritually, any idea that is in danger of conflicting with universal unity because it establishes standards of dualism and

---

1. Please refer to Hua-Ching Ni's version of the *I Ching: The Book of Changes and the Unchanging Truth*, SevenStar Communications, 1993.

partial-mindedness is a nuisance, unless it is used in a simple, common sense way in everyday life. Ideas should never be used to establish partiality. That was how once respectable cultures ran into trouble.

The Way is the universal spiritual way of Nature. It is the unformed subtle reality. The problem is, how does one help untrained, form-entrenched people respect the subtle and unformed universal spiritual reality?

Religious statues were designed to fulfill this function as intermediaries between the formed and unformed nature. Unfortunately, this good intention helped create religious dependency, and it is questionable whether this is beneficial or not. People become attached to symbols and forms. The use of statues contributes, to some degree, to religious manipulation of the Chinese, and particularly the Tibetans, both of whom are still encouraged to give offerings in exchange for blessings. This is why there was a need for the teachings of Zen (or "Chan" in Chinese) to supplement mainstream religious Buddhism. Zen encourages one to seek the internal spiritual reality rather than focus on external forms and structures.

The wise sage, Mohammed, abolished the worship of statues and forms in order to avoid all possible misunderstandings. After he ceased his physical life, the Muslim scholars, who had not achieved his level of spiritual stature, readopted the use of symbols in the new religion of Islam. Once again the worshippers of Islam became attached to symbols. In an attempt to help people move beyond form, the inner-spiritual tradition of Sufism was used to supplement Islam. But because Sufism is not really designed for the general public, the new clerics, most of whom were Sufis, began to compromise their spiritual conscience to the level of the masses. A similar situation occurred with Zen practitioners in Mahayana Buddhism.

Spiritually, formality is used for the masses; only a few individuals can enjoy the formless truth. Though this statement speaks to the challenges involved in uplifting people from the worship of forms to the unformed, Lao Tzu suggests keep working spiritually for the world as the fulfillment of your individual spiritual duty, but do not expect any result, especially quick results. As he directly stated, "*Wei Wu Wei*," which means, "just do it for that which cannot be achieved by doing." This statement can be understood more clearly when one considers that spiritual progress is related to the inner life of each individual, and that no one can live directly for another.

The disadvantage of the human mind is that it takes a long time to grow through its experiences. The prehistoric stage of human life covers over a million years. It was only around 8,000 years ago that humanity entered the cultural stage. In each stage, people could satisfy their real needs of life in one way or another. Around 3,000 years ago, new problems of religious struggle and competition arose. In response, many attempts and ideas have arisen in the hopes of bringing peace. Followers of the Integral Way, or Wayfarers, recognize that such efforts can be in vain. Instead, they recognize the importance and duty of self-cultivation in order to grow mentally and spiritually. Improving oneself is the most important mission in life.

Wayfarers of sound minds and sound spirits present the healthy and benign force of life. They hope to correct the worldly ideas, forms, and structures that are products of partially developed minds and spirits, and which have been mistakenly accepted by people as creations from achieved, whole minds.

Chapter 3

The Use of Consciousness

We humans are considered the highest form of life on Earth because of the subtle and refined conscious energy endowed to us by Mother Nature. Through consciousness we have an opportunity to connect with her. Mother Nature contains wavelengths of virtuous life energy, and she supports similar wavelengths of energy. She does not support less than virtuous wavelengths of energy. Therefore, connecting to Mother Nature depends on how we develop our consciousness and virtuous being.

Instinctually, we use our consciousness for self-protection and self-preservation. It can also be developed to bring forth knowledge in order to prevent the repetition of mistakes, to make positive progress, and to surpass the small ego self.

Spiritually, the conscious function is synonymous with responsibility, and being responsible establishes the dignity of human life in contrast to all other animals. Although animals possess similar functions to humans, these are not equal to the high consciousness of humans. Yet, despite the natural gift of consciousness, many do not develop or use it responsibly. Most prefer to behave like the lower animals, thus denying themselves the potential of developing a higher level of self-awareness. Self-awareness is what helps us establish a clear sense of responsibility in life. However, many people avoid this responsibility by following their emotions instead. That is when the conscious energy begins to separate from their life nature, opening the way for trouble.

Spiritual self-awareness is one notch higher than the general conscious capabilities such as thinking, though it is still a function of something else. Behind the conscious activities of our mind, and even behind our deep consciousness, is the spiritual energy of our life. This energy is the subtle, benign substance, or essence of our life. It is inexpressible, whereas the conscious energy, being expressible, is its spokesperson. The conscious activity of our mind, appearing as thoughts, ideas, imaginings and so forth, is the function or content of our mind, rather than the substance. And although our consciousness receives the effect of the spiritual substance, it usually ends up controlling and shaping that spiritual energy according to its own subjective conditioning, which, as we have mentioned, is a mix of healthy and unhealthy external conditioning, emotions, and desires.

When the spiritual energy appears as the self-awareness of our own trouble-making, it is a result of our alert mind's automatic ability to monitor our everyday life. However, we can consciously connect to a still deeper and higher department, which is our conscience or moral impulse.

The energy of the conscience expresses concern for the safety of our own life and other lives, as well as concern for the suitability of our behavior and life surroundings. The general conscious mind does not do that. When the conscience and the consciousness cooperate together, our life functions beyond the mere fulfillment of personal instinct and self-convenience to fulfill the extra duty of responsibility for one's family, society and even for the whole of humanity.

Throughout all spiritual functions, such as deep understanding, sympathy, humanistic love, and compassion, there is the wholeness of conscience. Once a human being has developed their spiritual functions, and can consciously express them in suitable ways, there has to be an equally great conscience as the root of one's moral behaviors. Such an individual is complete, and is no less than the macrouniverse. People of universal conscience treat all people as members of the one universal family. They are able to go beyond limiting concepts, and make a real and lasting contribution to the future of humanity.

Even though our conscience is valuable, indeed it is holy, we must continually engage in spiritual self-cultivation to purify our energies from the contamination of everyday life. A deep and objective understanding about the spiritual essence of Nature can only arise from a clear and pure consciousness. Heavy emotions and limiting beliefs distort the benign spiritual substance of our life. The purer and cleaner our mind and spirit, the closer we are to life's divinity.

In contrast, our emotions are more closely related to the physical experience of life, rather than the subtler conscious energy. Emotions are like vaporous sub-energies, whereas the conscious energy has more freedom. The conscious energy has the potential to freely exist at a distance from the physical being, while emotional energy can attach to the energy of our soul and remain as a memory, which is usually painful and can corrode our lives. When we overly identify with our emotions, rather than being guided by spiritual self-awareness, the conscious energy repeats our life's emotional pain, rather than helping us release or transform it. This is how we invite trouble and create our own hell.

After death, the lower souls retain the emotional experience longer than the conscious capability. The conscious emotional memory potentially can last three to seven times as long as the experience of life. Unfortunately, at death, the conscious energy can separate from the soul energy, when there is no brain function to support life. This can be a consequence of abusing the mind during life, as when overly associating with the emotions. The separation of the conscious energy from the soul energy is a serious loss to anyone, since to have conscious energy present is to be with the potential freedom of consciousness. The freedom of the conscious energy is not part of the lower life of the soul. In other words, it is not available to those who do not develop themselves. The freedom of the conscious energy can be attained through constructive spiritual cultivation and integration.

The content of our consciousness has the power to strengthen, weaken or misshape the spiritual energy of our life. Thus the resulting spiritual content may not be as pure as the original substance. The spiritual breadth of our life can therefore be limited or denied. This occurs, for example, when we shape our spiritual lives according to unhealthy emotions or conventional religious programs. Oftentimes people believe, mistakenly, that religious programs and teachings are the original spirituality when, in fact, those teachings are mere mental attempts to reach God as life's indescribable spiritual substance.

If you take a deep and objective look at religious and spiritual teachings, you will observe that most teachers have ignored the natural health of society, and the fluid, flexible, universal nature of spirituality itself. They have forced the souls of their generation and their descendants' generations to operate through limiting frameworks set by their own immature and partially developed conscious energy.

Many religious teachings were put together by individuals before they had fully explored and experienced the universal truth of life. Therefore, they have misinformed and influenced people with only a partial level of truth. Some teachings even operate for self-serving purposes. Those types of teachings fail to connect to the spiritual truth, remaining on the shallow and partial surface level. It therefore follows that such teachings would fail to serve people with a deep and balanced attitude in order to attain the basic goals of health, safety, and happiness.

There is no fault in attempting to reach God, but it is wrong to insist that one's particular attempts are the absolute or final truth. When your conscious energy imposes a narrow program on your spiritual energy, your spiritual sensitivity is dulled, and your spiritual potential is limited. If you program your life towards an unhealthy prejudice or hatred, the effects can even be deadly. The true spiritual reality of Nature is light and pure, whereas most worldly spiritual matters are heavy and impure. Heaviness implies that physical force is used, and impurity indicates an emotional blockage.

As natural energy, the soul cannot be destroyed, but its conscious content of life experience, which people hold up as the life of the self, can be lost. If the connection of the conscious content of life experience is severed from the natural energy of the soul, it is a permanent loss and means that the life has been wasted.

Rather than limit or disconnect from the spiritual substance of our lives by adhering to emotional and psychological experiences, we can use our experiences to grow and develop our conscious energy and fortify our spiritual energy. This is the purpose of self-cultivation, and is our spiritual duty as guided by the teachings of the Integral Way. The Integral Way helps people improve their mental and emotional conditions through open, objective spiritual learning, and through the pursuit of the five healths of mental, physical, spiritual, moral, and financial health. From such a healthy foundation, we are more receptive and better equipped to pursue objectively the deep spiritual wisdom of life, and to serve others.

The current conflicts in the world cannot be solved using tools created from our conceptual minds. New choices and real solutions come from clear and effective visions, which, in turn, come from the developed perceptual power of individuals who maintain a natural, pure consciousness and conscience.

Chapter 4

The New Direction of Human Progress

Around 6,000 to 8,000 years ago, in the early humanistic culture of the Way, the early Chinese people held the view that the Sky and the Earth were the parents of their lives. Heaven was their father, Earth was their mother, and all human beings were siblings. This view was based on their pure and direct perceptions of Nature. It was an essentially healthy and integral view of life that did not invite self-doubt or discrimination towards others. The world was considered one family that emphasized humanistic love.

At the same time, people in the Middle East viewed themselves and Nature as creations of a single Creator, who made them not by hand but by will. This kind of omnipotent will power was a projection of the human mind onto Nature in order to make Nature more understandable. However, Nature does not function like the human mind. A mind can only create reproductions or rearrangements of existing external conditions, whereas Nature is self-creating and requires no preexisting conditions. The mind alone cannot make anything happen; it can only affect other minds that are similar to itself.

For social and religious purposes, this "Creator" was portrayed as a male, with overly-emphasized masculine characteristics. As different religious sects began to develop in this area of the world, the Creator was conceived differently, and conflicts inevitably developed between different faiths. Those conflicts led to discrimination against fellow human beings, and even to threats against their survival.

Originally, the human conception of God as a masculine entity may have been a way of honoring or complementing Mother Nature. On the other hand, around 3,000 years ago it may also have been a way to facilitate the transition from a matriarchal to a patriarchal culture. Whatever the case may be, human society has become mentally tighter and more rigidly disciplined since then, due mostly to the concept of a Creator being nothing more than a conception of the human mind. A conception has no ability to create the world or life. To maintain belief in a concept requires unwavering faith and discipline in the face of the daily realities of Nature, which is continually evolving herself from the raw material of existence.

If one stops to examine the process of creation by the human mind, it is clearly an externalization of an internal image. You could say there are two stages. First, the internal creation, which then gives birth to the external creation that then results in something that separates from the "parent." This new and separate creation is part of the natural life expression of its "creator" or source. It is similar to the creation of a story by an author.

Now, does Nature possess a mind, or does the mind simply reflect the creativity of Nature? No mind can exist prior to physical life. Human perception, in the purest and most uncontaminated sense, is not a creation. It is the result of passively receiving whatever exists, and then being able to clearly and directly relate that perception. How is this relevant? Those who believe in "Creation" should actively and openly utilize their daily contact with Nature as the foundation of their religious faith. Nature is the foundation of the human concept of "God." God is simply a manicured image that makes the reality of Nature more accessible and acceptable to the human mind.

If human faith can be linked to Nature, the integration of science and religion can occur. Nature is integral. Science, the child of the human mind, is segmented. Nature expresses itself by evolving from oneness to multiplicity. Science expresses itself by evolving from multiplicity to oneness. Those who only look at the forest can lose sight of the single tree. Those who only look at the single tree are unable to see the whole forest. The Integral Way, expressed through the balanced human mind, bridges apparent conflicts such as these and reduces confrontation. In ancient Chinese culture, it is said that the myriad things can return to the oneness of their same source, just as that source embraces the myriad things and all lives that are created by it.

Chapter 5

Achieving Great Spiritual Success

Achieving spiritual success begins with helping people appreciate the power of their natural mental and spiritual functions. At the very least, people should be guided to discern between what is useful and what is not useful in their lives. Doing so naturally involves becoming more spiritually and materially self-reliant. With self-reliance, one can attain true growth through real experience.

When we rely on governments and religions to tell us how to live, and on all sorts of convenient products and expert services to do things for us, we neglect how to do things for ourselves. This is particularly so in matters relating to our physical and spiritual health. Consequently, our inner abilities remain undeveloped. In caring for our life and in matters of spiritual growth, the only person who can truly be trusted is oneself.

By this we do not mean that we should live apart from society, since very few do. A self-reliant spirit works together with society, and since society is made up of individuals, improving the quality of each individual is a priority. The priority above all priorities, though, is the deepening spiritual growth of people. For this to occur, we need to develop our own lives and keep away from the unhealthy knowledge of society. Only from a clean mind can we passively perceive life and understand what is useful and what is not. We can then save ourselves from the trouble of external reliance.

The high power of understanding comes from the power of direct perception. This power leads to deep vision and wisdom about life, and helps one avoid troubles. It is not the same as general intelligence or general observation. Rather, it is the ability to observe sensitively and objectively, and to comprehend life in all its subtlety, with or without the support of mechanical instruments.

The power of direct perception does not rely on academic ability or book learning, though these pursuits can help us to express ourselves. Their disadvantage is that they tend to block the mind's natural perceptual and reflective functions. Through the bare mind, we can perceive, discover and intuit, as well as express business and political acumen. Just look at how Edison and Einstein achieved themselves, as well as self-made bosses who are more capable than their college-educated employees. With an open, bare mind, we can perceive far more than those whose perceptions have been colored and blocked by the intellectual mind.

In ancient China, people relied on nothing else but the development of their natural mind and spirit. Confidence in the bare mind came from individuals who engaged in the pursuit of spiritual immortality. Through their direct perception of Nature, they came to a deep and integral understanding about the subtle functioning of the universe, the world, and personal life. They used this under-standing to support their unusually long and healthy lives. There was no help from modern nutrition or external medicine. It is appropriate to commemorate them for their objective and matter-of-fact attitude and achievements. Their understandings were gathered and have been passed down through thousands of years.

The body of wisdom became known as the "Way," and its followers known as "Wayfarers." It was eventually passed down to our family, the Ni family. Today it is known as the Integral Way. The Way continues to be revealed through the power of direct perception of life. The Way shares its secrets with all those who choose to live in harmony with its depths.

Wayfarers present the deep and plain humanistic understanding of life. They do not insist on their views, and their teaching does not contain any fixed dogma. They freely offer their deep insights to help the world and fulfill the duty of a natural, healthy life without harming anyone. Wayfarers cannot be defined as holy or divine. Essentially, their life is an expression of the mental power that keeps them safe from the harm of greed and insistence.

The integral and flexible views of the Wayfarers are very different than the limited conceptual views of later religions, and the segmented, mechanistic views of science. These views can obstruct the power of human perception by shaping it to fit narrow and partial interpretations. The universality of the Way, how-ever, is able to coexist with both science and religion, despite the fact that these later systems are unable to find harmony between themselves. The Way is also able to deepen the interconnection between religious faiths, and assist science by modifying its extremes.

Here are some examples of the universal wisdom produced from the achieved ancestors, who applied their power of perception to phenomena.

When the power of perception was applied to Nature, Fu Shi (3852–2738 BCE) discovered the system of changes of *yin* and *yang*, and the principle of appropriateness in worldly life. The two energies or forces of *yin* and *yang* became the foundation for the 64 energetic patterns (or hexagrams as recorded in the *I Ching*) that can be used to describe the energetic qualities of all phenomena. By measuring any event or situation against these different patterns, we can perceive whether the events are balanced or not. This system helps us to understand the energetic laws behind any situation or phenomenon.

When the power of perception was applied to plants, Shen Nung (3218–2078 BCE) discovered their value for food and health. When the power is applied to health problems, the Yellow Emperor (2698–2598 BCE) envisioned the great principle of balance in developing remedies for people's health issues. His work formed the foundation of traditional Chinese medicine.

When applied to the ruling system of the day, King Wen (1766–1121 BCE) conceived of a benevolent and useful political initiative to help improve the social culture, and replace the tyrannical rule of King Jow. When applied to physical competition, Sun Tze (544–496 BCE) developed a strategy of using efficient force to reduce the brutality in physical conflict and war. He perceived a strategy for victory that involved little or no fighting; thereby preventing the loss of life.

When applied to the ways of working life, Fang Rei (who was born around 245 BCE) developed commerce as a completely new style of life-making, whereby people could work individually and peacefully with the material aspects of society. He encouraged people to find their own strength and discipline, rather than rely on the government. Several times he amassed great wealth, and each time he gave it away. He paved the way for a society of self-reliant individuals and a cooperative government that did not overly interfere with, or overly tax its people. Fang Rei combined practical life improvement as encouraged by the Yellow Emperor, with Lao Tzu's spiritual attitude of giving away that which is over and above what one needs.

When the power of deep perception is applied to spiritual problems, there is no other way but to develop the Integral Way. Today, the Integral Way offers solutions to problems at all levels of life by helping people find a cooperative balance between worldly materialistic life and inner spiritual growth.

In my traditional education of the Way, the word "function" was replaced by the word "virtue," which means the healthy functioning of life in all aspects. For example, people generally think in terms of what they are able to do and achieve. In our tradition, we think about what we are able to do in a naturally whole and healthy-minded way, without crookedness or self-deception. We trust the natural, healthy abilities of life.

If you would like to develop your natural, spiritual abilities in order to serve your life, you first need to understand what it means to be spiritually-minded. The spiritually developed minds of the ancient ones were naturally detached, independent, and objective. It is this quality of mind that opens itself to perceiving visions that can help one's life. These visions are not the same as a set of products produced from certain ideas. Rather, these visions come about by nurturing the ability to perceive the depth of any person or situation. A neutral or unaffected mind is able to accurately reflect the subtle functions of the spiritual sphere of human life. It can also help you evolve to the high level of universal spiritual reality. But before going too high too soon, let me begin with some simple examples of using the natural mind.

People who respect their natural minds can know things without the need of external instruments. For example, they know whether they have gained weight without the need of weighing instruments, or they know the condition of their internal organs by simply feeling the subtle pulse of their blood vessels without the need of a blood pressure device. Proof of spiritual functioning can also be found in such a common situation as thinking of someone and having the phone ring with the person you are thinking about on the line. This occurs because when you wonder about something, you unconsciously reach out to it. Another common example is when you have a question in your mind, and you randomly open a book to find the answer is written right in front of you. These are just a few examples. You may have other experiences depending on your stage of development.

It is also possible to develop foreknowledge and attain the power of self-knowledge. These subtle functions are very different from what you see produced in hypnosis or magic shows. It is also different from the effects of using crystal balls, candlelight and so forth, to evoke the power of inner sight. By quieting your mind, and observing the subtle messages within your own body and surroundings, you can practically and effectively serve your life without over-relying on external instruments.

The spiritual energy of your life is natural. It just needs guidance from an objective and balanced teaching that helps you to understand and experience the whole truth of what you are. Unfortunately, most of you do not pay attention to your spiritual energy, or you consider it too remote and unreachable. Its existence therefore escapes you. You may also limit its potential by ignorantly bending your mind to a partial system of thought, such as an unbalanced political or religious program.

The key to genuinely and deeply understanding the mystery of spirituality is at your fingertips. You only need to know how to unlock the door.

The ancient Chinese sage and wayfarer Chuang Tzu (ca. 275 BC), used metaphor to describe what to do when you face a sealed secret or problem of life. By using the metaphor of a butcher carving up the carcass of a cow, he explained how to prepare your mind (the knife) to open the secret or event (the cow) without damaging your mind or the information. You can then receive the information in all its wholeness.

He explains that whatever you face in life, there is a natural course to it, and that the "eyes" of your mind face the challenge of finding it. He advises that it is more important to find the clues with your inner vision before using your physical strength. The inexperienced butcher does not know where to begin, so he uses his knife roughly on the skin of the carcass. He is unable to separate the meat neatly and effortlessly. In contrast, the specially achieved butcher is able to "see" the cracks and holes in the sinews of the carcass. He is thus able to use his knife effectively to separate easily the meat from the skin and bones without dulling or damaging his knife.

Looking at Nature, human society, or the events of one's life like the whole cow in the metaphor, you can know where and how to apply the strength of your mind (the knife) with its powers of perception and inner vision. By calmly and deeply observing the whole situation rather than a small part, you can find a place to put your knife and open it up thoroughly.

Almost every person has their own "cow" (life event or social challenge) to cut open. It needs to be cut open neatly so that your "knife" (the mind) does not damage your "hand" (life). The duty to perform a clean and neat job applies not only to your own life, but to any event of the world.

What Chuang Tzu is saying is that the subtle laws of Nature are in everything. By quieting the mind and cultivating special vision, one can see these laws operating in the world, in the events of life, in Nature and in the nature of one's own life. Those with experienced eyes can detect the "cracks and holes" to help break through all types of life's riddles.

Chuang Tzu places value on developing special vision that requires a process of observation and subtle skill in dealing with events and problems. He emphasizes looking for and seeing clues before raising your hand. The young and inexperienced face an important duty to ensure the job is well done. One must be dutiful in becoming self-responsible and self-reliant for the work of life.

The metaphor had real significance some three to four thousand years ago in China, when it was customary for the leaders to sacrifice a cow in gratitude to Heaven and Earth for the grace and protection given to people. The royal butcher was responsible for cutting up the beef into equal portions for distribution to the different communal families. If the proportion was not equal, it could be taken as a sign of disrespect, and an argument would ensue. Therefore, the even distribution of social wealth was a great responsibility.

However, life is not always as simple as carving up meat and distributing it equally. In life, we need to be aware of how we serve life. We should first be aware that the mind is a tool that can easily be damaged if used carelessly. Therefore, learning the Way is not about making emotion or external information the lord of our life. It is about developing ourselves mentally and spiritually in order to face and manage life's challenges with serenity and wisdom. The Way is not about preparing the way to go to Heaven, but rather about developing a universal, humanistic approach that seeks objective wisdom and the way of natural consequences in living life.

Most people, especially the young and inexperienced, use physical or emotional force to try to pry open social doors to make a living. Consequently, they end up emotionally wounding themselves, or "denting their knife." This can be very discouraging. However, for those who sincerely develop themselves, and who grow patiently and wisely through difficulties, the rewards will come.

As Chuang Tzu suggests when facing a challenge, do not panic or run away, but take the time to calm yourself and observe the whole situation carefully and objectively. You can then find the safe and appropriate way to proceed. The high Way is effortlessly or easily achieved, while the low way uses might and achieves poor results.

Our world is overflowing with information and organized knowledge on numerous subjects, many of which have been packed into the academic pursuits of young lives. Yet, even though the young minds are stuffed with concepts, and their mouths full of words in order to receive remuneration and respect as experts, those things cannot help produce the power of spiritual perception.

It is not physical force, emotional force or even intellectual force that helps us find the solutions we need to live a healthy life, or achieve spiritual success. Rather, it is the power of direct perception. The thick walls of intellectual knowledge and cloudy emotional energy only ruin our spiritual sensitivity, and block us from experiencing subtle messages. Without the power of perception, we end up a mere intellectual or emotional slave of our conditioned life.

Once we appreciate our inner spiritual strength, we begin to follow a different pursuit. We recognize that spiritual strength becomes something to cultivate, rather than just a faith or belief to occupy the mind.

Spiritual development requires a foundation of self-training. You can begin any time with a simple spiritual goal and discipline, such as studying the principles of the *I Ching* to nurture the sensitivity of knowing your own, or another's intentions and feelings.

The power of perception is the real teacher of humanity. It helps us to walk away from all types of self-created problems, which manifest as limiting conceptual beliefs and which are the cause of the world's troubles. When the developed mental power of perception is used to serve human health, people will naturally understand Nature. Then they will no longer busily adhere to their mentally created beliefs. The deep power of perception is a worthy endeavor to pursue in any field.

Chapter 6

The Spiritually Empowered Personality

We humans are not an isolated phenomenon in the universe; we are a part of Nature. Nature affects us and we affect Nature, such as when we damage our natural surroundings through irresponsible behavior. This is not wise. What is wise is learning to live deeply connected to Mother Nature.

In our human world, we have set up a lot of laws and regulations to help us conduct our lives because we have neglected our sense of personal responsibility and management. In the process, we ignore the subtle laws which exist universally and which govern the deep sphere of our lives and destiny. Destiny is related to how we shape ourselves, moment to moment, through our thoughts and behaviors. By quietly and objectively observing life, we can begin to reconnect to Nature and her subtle laws. We can spiritually develop our minds, so that we can read Nature's subtle messages and enlarge our being to communicate with the universe. All we need do is to stop separating ourselves from Nature by foolishly and improperly competing with her, and attune to her natural network instead. Our life is then supported by the universal nature through a new center of universal connection.

Unlike people, animals and birds do not rely on intellectual knowledge to make decisions. They rely on a preinstalled, instinctual system of knowledge that can be observed, for instance, in the migratory patterns of birds and sea life. It is marvelous to see that most animals can preempt a natural disaster much faster than we can, despite our technologically advanced detection devices. Frogs, for example, know the coming of a storm, and horses have been known to return home from a battlefield covering distances of thousands of miles. Animals have not forsaken their connection to Nature.

Most of us, however, disrespect those lives which have a lower, or no conscious sense of life. We have become overly proud of our conscious and descriptive abilities, describing things in ways that are much more than the reality of the thing itself. Yet, as part of Nature, each of us is endowed with spiritual energy, and has the potential to commune deeply with the natural reality. Individuals who remain attuned to Nature, and who develop the spiritual mind, can receive subtle messages from natural creations such as trees and flowers. This is called natural inspiration. Unfortunately, many of us are not able to receive the messages because we ignore and disrespect our connection to Nature.

Once we lose the ability to read Nature's messages, there is no teacher, healer, preacher or religion that can restore our connection. On the contrary, our mind only becomes more confused by the stories and concepts that trap it in a particular religious framework, and which cause us to lose objectivity. How can we then be expected to develop an open mind and self-reliant spirit? True help comes through the genuine response of our inner spirits, which are our naturally endowed spiritual power. When we connect to and strengthen our inner spiritual power, we can restore our connection to Nature and enjoy its true support. Out of all the spiritual teachings of humanity, however, very few carry this message.

With Mother Nature's help, it is possible to enhance the mind and recover our natural common sense and spiritual abilities. Self-recovery requires us to avoid or reduce emotional indulgence, unnecessary hassles, and the rigid conceptions of modern life. It is better to transfer our focus, or at least a portion of it, away from spiritually insignificant things such as television, newspapers, and magazines to observing things of Nature. There, we can discover natural teachings and natural cures. We can pick up impressions about things that we may have generally overlooked. Deep spiritual meaning can be shaped from repeated natural impressions. It was through the deep observation of Nature that the quiet-minded individuals of ancient China developed their understanding of universal laws. Over time, those great individuals gathered together their common understandings, and presented them as universal spiritual messages to people, some of which are written down below.

Mother Nature teaches through inspiration rather than words or concepts. She expresses herself through her natural creations. You may wonder how you can pick up Nature's messages when she is so large and scattered. It comes about through the Subtle Law of Correspondence or Similarity, and it touches the most sincere heart. Even when the phenomenon that provides you with the inspiration is not directly related to what you want to know, your spiritual mind touches upon a similar characteristic that is needed to give you the inspiration for your inquiry. For instance, when you are wondering about something or someone, you may hear about, or see something or someone that resembles the matter you wish to know about. It usually occurs when you are calm and quiet-minded. If you search for a message with too much force or intensity, your emotion or expectation will block or disturb the flow of energy through the subtle network. The message is then distorted or interrupted. With a bare, quiet mind you can receive messages anywhere, even in a car park or on a busy street. You just need to set your mind in neutral, or the "zero dimension."

Individuals of high spiritual character possess an internal value of life rather than an external value. Such individuals are able to produce spiritual power, read subtle signs, and hear spiritual messages. They use these functions as their spiritual support and encouragement alongside their regular life activities. Because they live with the spiritual network of the universe, they recognize that they are never spiritually isolated. By attuning yourself to the universal network, you can also prove that you live a universal life, and that the universe is you and you are the universe. The performance of miracles is not your pursuit, but by spiritually communicating with Mother Nature you will know that she will never abandon you, because you are one with her.

The ancient developed ones wish us to know that the Mother Universe is reachable. In order to reach her spiritual nature, we need to achieve the universal mind. This can be done by removing all false images and illusions from the mind, and by nurturing the universal heart of life. After achieving the universal mind, we will discover that there is no separation between us, other people, and Mother Nature. We will also be able to receive messages from Nature, which will help us to update the spiritual condition of our lives continuously.

The Message of the Sun

The sun supports human life. It is an expression of the spiritual health and prosperity of human life. Spiritually, its energy represents the life source of every person. A useful and healthy practice is to be like the bright light of the sun. In ancient times, the sun symbolized confidence in life, and was considered an example of how to live one's life on Earth.

A safe and healthy amount of sunlight benefits our physical well-being, and enhances the spiritual sphere of our life. Sunlight can lift a person out of depression, and strengthen a weak spiritual condition. The secret of a healthy, enduring life and an immortal soul is related to the secrets of the sun.

If you have an open mind, you can find examples of healthy attributes and moral characteristics in natural phenomena. Below, are nine natural phenomena each of which exhibit a healthy characteristic, and represent the spirituality of Mother Nature. These spiritual characteristics can be shaped and developed. They are aspects of the complete spiritual character of universal life that we, ourselves, can become.

竣 德 如 山
The Message of the Mountains

山德:信
=无欺,
不不,
不他惑.
不去惑人.

Mother Nature's spiritual message via the mountains
　is that the morality of life should be upheld,
　　just like the mountains uphold themselves.
The mountains express the trustworthiness of Nature,
　and stand for the spirit of honesty.
They are neither shaken nor puzzled by others,
　nor do they engage in temptation.
Why don't you learn from the mountains?
They have been sent by Mother Nature to teach you.

含 德 如 海
The Message of the Seas

海德:容受
=大度容受
无所敌对
深藏广蓄
益万方

The seas uphold the moral nature of the one great ocean as the mother of all lives.
Tolerance is the hallmark of the great ocean.
All seas accept things with tolerance.
They hold no hostility towards anyone.
In their depths, they shelter and nurture a variety of lives,
    and protect them from being exposed.
Can you open your eyes and see the multiple benefits and teachings of the seas?

德 如 川
The Message of the Rivers

川德
=不拒流
从善如流
川流不息
不存垢

The rivers are moral.
They do not refuse any small flow of water,
    and accept whatever advice is offered.
They never cease flowing, and they do not gather dirt.
You should learn from the rivers, instead of being superstitious.

德 如 松

The Message of the Pine Trees

松德
不畏高,但喜月明,
虽求勇健,不求特.

The moral nature of the pine trees is such
   that they have no fear.
They are not afraid of severe winds,
   though they prefer them when in the company of the bright moon.
With their roots, they do not look for special nutrition,
   only a firm and constant hold.
Can you see there is something to learn from these trees?

德 如 柏

The Message of the Cypress Trees

柏德:固
任他雪,
我不折腰.
任他蔓天白,
我青不改.

The moral nature of the cypress is chastity.
Although they allow the snow to suppress their head,
   they refuse to bend to power or force.
While the whole world may chase after the new fashion of being clad in white,
   they remain evergreen.
Are you missing something in times of adversity?

德 如 竹
The Message of the Bamboo

竹德
自制:可可,可雅可俗;
虽其通，但持有.

The moral nature of the bamboo is temperance.
It does not care whether you see it as noble or not,
    for it is flexible and self-principled.
From its example, can you learn to be open-minded,
    self-reliant, and helpful to the world?

德 如 莲
The Message of the Lotus Flowers

德
自洁 =
不惧泥,不染泥
自能高洁，待人言.

The moral characteristic of the lotus flower is self-cleanliness.
Absorbed by its beauty, however,
    people generally overlook this quality.
Because of its self-clean nature,
    the lotus has no fear of mud, since mud cannot soil its character.
Despite their superior, clean nature they do not incline to flattery.
From their example, can you learn to attain a clean
    and beautiful character in spite of your experience of the muddy world?

静 德 如 兰

The Message of the Orchids

德
自静自安,自自适,
有香不烈,不去人.

If orchids could proclaim themselves, they would say,
   we are able to establish our own model as the moral nature of the orchid.
We are happy and peaceful in quiet and lonely places,
   and though we can produce a fragrance, it is not for attraction,
   it is simply what we are.
For our beauty, you gather us from the deep mountains and dangerous, high cliffs.
But, aside from our attractiveness,
   can you notice the subtle, spiritual character of our lives?

善 德 如 菊

The Message of the Chrysanthemums

菊德
有自信,信善美,
善能自任,矢志完成.

You may have neglected the moral characteristics of the chrysanthemums.
They live with confidence and faith in the health and beauty of their own lives.
They take responsibility for their own beauty,
   and accomplish their lives despite intimidating, cold frosts.

(Any individual who is able to hear or read, and be spiritually encouraged by the living messages that come from their natural surroundings is truly wise and spiritual.)

全 德 大 美
C o m p l e t e   V i r t u e

有类太窄,
玫瑰与牡丹,
桃李郁金香,
何以不入类?
或香,
人称富.
虽人所羡,
凭气和暖.
与依,
不属於清流.
不富与,
但取人与品.

You may say that these nine examples are not broad enough.
There are many other flowers like roses, peonies,
　　tulips, peaches, and white plums.
Why haven't they been considered?
The overly showy are not chosen,
　　because like noble and rich people,
　　who are admired and attended to by many,
　　their achievement comes from the ample support of the warm seasons
　　and wet soil, rather than their own inner, spiritual strength.
In life, it is your spiritual strength that can be relied upon,
　　rather than money and social power.
Showy and sweetly scented flowers cannot endure the frost, ice, and snow,
　　so they do not deserve to be spiritually admired.
In choosing spiritual examples, it is not the easy life of
　　the rich and noble that is exemplified.
It is the character and strength of a high moral nature that is admired.

常流如蔓草,
宴倒依向.
性型不明,
奸邪藏其中.

Generally, people are like grasses
    that bend in any wind.
Among big groups of people, characters are difficult to clearly distinguish,
    so it is easy for the wicked and cunning to hide.

九品台做佛,
九品中正官.
莫品德不,
天下滔滔无德多.

The priests from Mahayana Buddhism used the nine levels
    of the Lotus Flower as bait to lure people to Buddhism.
Rulers from the Han Dynasty used the nine official ranks
    to attract people to serve them.
You may think that the power of people's characters is not worth anything.
Yet observe the state of the world, where most people are immoral.

天下宗教常流,
所崇圣是人.
天神仙佛皆,
那及自然九气真.
山川花木譬人格.
取象九品自然.
宇宙真性露形迹,
万象列性独真.

Religions of the world tempt people,
  and worship human-made creations.
But understand that all heavenly beings, angels, and buddhas are mere metaphors.
They are hardly as truthful as the nine natural characteristics of
  spiritual power demonstrated in a completely developed personality.
The mountains, seas, rivers, trees, and flowers mentioned above
  are symbols of great personalities.
Those nine things present the deep and natural truth.
They are the traces of the true universal nature.
Yet, despite her displays of multiple phenomena,
  Mother Nature maintains her freedom above all.

大德似若全,
有德似无德.
大成若缺.
大巧若拙.
大智若愚.
大有若不足.
全德若.

The greatly virtuous appears unaccomplished and lacking in virtue.
The greatly accomplished appears incomplete.
The great craftsperson appears clumsy.
The great, wise one looks like a fool.
The greatest possession appears insufficient.
Those complete in virtue appear as if there is something missing.

天地有非灾,
日月有晦.
海上浪,
山上有峻壁,
川有壅滞,

泛即成灾.
却成其,
自入圣.

Even the sky and Earth incur unexpected troubles.
The sun and moon have times that are not so bright.
The great ocean can experience strong winds and turbulent waves,
　　and the great mountains occasionally encounter steep cliffs.
Sometimes rivers become stuck,
　　and sometimes they overflow.
Yet no matter what you encounter,
　　always refuse evil and accomplish good.
This is the true way to join ranks with the sages.

全德不立型,
气性仍有,
依而辨型,
仍在九类中.

Although Complete Virtue cannot be cast in a mold,
　　there are certain inclinations from which moral characters
　　may be distinguished.
Yet, they still belong to the commonplace types.

虽可'全德,'
全德似无德,
当称'德.'
德乃德.
德是大善.
当其一.
人自辨,
友人可代.

Although Complete Virtue is recognizable,
   it resembles lack of virtue.
Still, it should be termed "Hidden Virtue."
Now, Hidden Virtue is virtue that is pure and modest.
And Modest Virtue is ultimately compassionate.
When one is challenged or confronted, one such should be chosen.
Yet, it is difficult for people to distinguish it in themselves,
   so good friends can help you see and choose.

天下学不能全，
只有品德堪依仗.
中西文化果然高，
孰是珍珠孰大米?

No one possesses all branches of knowledge,
   but you can rely on the character of some.
Observing the achievements of the East and the West,
   which among them are the pearls, and which are the rice?

全呈献已无余，
藏珍珠大米.
宇宙大母宗教，
修品德藏宝珠.

I have presented a sketch of complete spiritual knowledge.
Hide the pearls in your bosom, but sell the rice.
The Mother Universe is the new religion,
   and cultivating virtue is the pearl to hide.

天神地祗怎堪?
人之品性尚堪凭.
品德修靠教,
友砥砺不可无.

No one can depend on the divine intervention of Heaven and Earth,
   but you can rely on the character of some people.
Uplifting the moral character of people depends on a good,
   constructive teaching, which can only be offered through the help
   of sincere and reliable teachers and friends.

自然大母作宗教,
教会化成砺德.
道德信仰化成一,
内外合修德乃全.

The Mother Universe is the religion of the universe.
The new centers and churches that grow up in her name
   should be places that nurture the high moral power
   and constructive character of people.
By combining the internal effort to achieve high moral power
   with a natural and constructive spiritual education,
   people can complete themselves.

Chapter 7

The Spiritual Truth is Integral

In the classification of substance and function, substance is the truth and functions are also the truth. Among the functions, there are healthy or normal functions and unhealthy and subnormal functions. As to substance, there is the recognition of what type of quality to differentiate that it is unformed material, or a formed product or creation. As a creation, there is a quality and a level of craftsmanship, both of which present a fact or a truth to our minds.

Spirituality is the nature, or substance, of the material sphere of life. How that nature is presented or functions through the material life is at the disposal of the mind to recognize or use. In a sense, spirituality cannot be separated from the material.

The mind is the functional aspect of human life. It cannot be separated from the physical life. Our minds are partly expressible, and partly inexpressible or hidden. Together, these parts form the whole or complete mind.

The hidden aspect of the mind is the source of spirituality. It is a spiritual storehouse of the natural world, containing the spirits of our lives. However, most people mistakenly perceive the spirits to be separate beings outside of their lives. Conventional religious teachers base their teachings on this view, believing that the spiritual function of life is separate and different from the reality of life. Consequently, many religious followers remain ignorant about the spiritual truth.

If we deeply explore and spiritually develop our life, we will discover that life itself is the true religion. There is no spiritual government in the sky, but there are spiritual functions deep within our life. Our mind and body are the storehouse of spirits. The spirits are benign. They do not have emotions, or likes and dislikes as the mind does, but because they operate like a reflective system, they can be influenced by the quality, emotion, and personality of one's mind. Therefore, if there is fear in the mind, the spirits will reflect a fearful image. So the spirits can be godly or devilish depending on how we summon them through our thoughts and actions. We all have the spiritual capability to draw out an angel or a monster; it depends on how we treat ourselves and one another. This is the reality of life before we develop spiritually.

Conventional religions were designed to bring out God, or godly qualities, from the life of their believers. But, by overly emphasizing the difference between God and the devil, the two became active in worldly life. When God is raised high, the devil is pressed down low, bringing about the unexpected result that both are established. Therefore, any benefit religions may have given to society is at least fifty percent off its mark since once you call out God from life, the devil is called out at the same time. Some religious teachers consider divisions such as God and the devil, holy and unholy, to be permanent. This dualistic approach was used to support other human-made concepts. It came about after people lost touch with their ability to perceive life integrally and objectively, and without any psychological or mental distortion.

In Asian spiritual traditions, there is a saying that when you raise the good of God as high as one foot, the evil of the devil creates an obstacle of ten feet to deter your one foot of good interest. This describes the spiritual obstacles one may face from the mind when spiritually cultivating. That is why we suggest you live with an integral mind, and allow the spiritual functions of your life to respond spontaneously to situations. There is no need to bring out God, and invite the devil at the same time. Lao Tzu described it as *"Wu Wei,"* which essentially means not to do anything extra or beyond what is naturally suitable or adequate in situations.

The deep truth about life and spirituality is that it is integral; it is complete and whole. Any separation into parts, such as holy and unholy, is superficial and potentially misleading. Unfortunately, separating things is still the common, foolish behavior of most people who are trained by concepts that twist their natural minds.

All truths are one truth. When you exalt the absolute truth as the high truth, you lower other levels of truth. The genuine truth has to be complete with all levels of truth. The partial exaltation of any level of truth means to take advantage of something or someone, and this is untruthful. For example, if you raise the spiritual side of life high so as to suppress or disrespect the secular side of life (which includes being financially self-supporting), you are asking for a donation to support your, or someone else's particular lifestyle. Spiritual development means to develop your whole life. It is not about raising one part of life higher than another. This only leads to separation and an unhealthy life.

After experiencing the deep level of life, it is clear to me that all human creations, customs, laws, social, religious and political organizations, are mostly established for the purpose of smoothing out conflicts and establishing order among people. These relate to the external level of life rather than the deep spiritual truth. As the children of Mother Nature we should no longer be confused by the external level, which provides only a limited service. All seeking through religion, science, philosophy and emotion, attempt to give answers about life, but most focus on the superficial, external level.

Real spiritual practice involves deepening our spiritual awareness, and aligning our life to the healthy, benign essence of Nature's spiritual sphere. A spiritually balanced mind is closer to the Truth than any partial explanation or worship. The worship of words and concepts block us from experiencing the spiritual reality of life. The best practice for us is to embrace the goodwill of natural life, and the highest power of magic that we can perform is to treat all we encounter as God. These practices will bring genuine reward.

The ultimate truth of life is one. Therefore, you should give up the partial approaches and superficial facts based on shallow observations, dialectic and dualistic thinking, and emotional beliefs. Human knowledge and its creations should be respected, but in the light of the truth of oneness, you recognize human knowledge for the external level of what it is. It is then no longer mistaken for the deep, subtle matters of life.

I encourage you all to go deeper, and listen to the Integral Truth of Nature through the uncontaminated perception of your integral, intuitive mind. You may then meet the whole Truth that is above observation and thinking conditioned by time, location, education, and maturity of the acquired mind.

The intuitive mind, however, usually receives an impression of the whole picture without words. Therefore, the question becomes, "What can we establish as a common understanding that all advanced minds can agree upon?" For this we need to use the whole mind with all of life's spiritual functions. Since the whole mind takes time to cultivate and develop though, what can be the reliable truth for now?

I recommend the teachings of the Integral Way. These teachings present the essence of the Integral Truth as passed down by the developed minds of the immortal pursuers from ancient China. The Integral Truth contains the past, present, and future in the sense of time, and it contains all directional and dimensional development, as well as the deep potential of life. In the Integral Truth, nothing is left out, and nothing can be further divided. It is simply the wholeness of universal life.

Through cultivating the Way of Integral Truth, you can dissolve the duality in life and find unity. You can go beyond the superficial, external level where the believers and God, and the nonbelievers and God are considered separate, to the Integral Truth where they are all one. It is a way of being where the observer and the observed have merged, and the thinker and the thoughts have converged. What then is there to pursue, overcome and conquer? Such attitudes and their consequent troubles are all a result of focusing on the superficial, segmented levels of life, rather than on the whole. The Way of the Integral Truth guides you to go beyond the partial evaluation of life to the deep level of the whole truth.

The only safe and wholesome spiritual practice is to embrace the Way of the Mother Universe, as she does not exercise any partial beliefs or partial explanations. The practice of the Integral Truth is that whatever you do, whether big or small, it should be done exactly right, and every day of your life should be spent completely balanced. As an old saying goes, "Do not think a good thing is so small that you do not do it, and do not think an evil thing is so small that you do it anyway."

Chapter 8

The Open Truth of the Mother of All Truth

Who or what else is able to give away all truths other than the Mother Universe?

It is both interesting and laughable that through generations humans have engaged in artificial, ideological competition, calling the creation of their ideas "culture." Truthfully, we humans have confused ourselves. We no longer recognize our own faces after painting them with so many colors and designs. Should any kind-hearted person add more confusion by creating new objects of worship? At least I am disciplined not to create new mischief, working instead to guide my fellow humans back to the plain nature of the Mother Universe. Is she not the source of all truth?

Our human life faces a common difficulty. We know that we are a different kind of animal, which needs a ruling image in our lives, otherwise we tend to cause trouble for ourselves. That was what motivated various leaders to initially engage in the creation of ideas and images so as to create order in their surroundings. This was effective for a time. Today, societies have opened up to one another on a global scale. We have become one big society. Humanity now faces the problem of choosing a culture that is more appropriate as a common faith in a world of global interaction and interrelationship.

The ancient ancestors of China seemed to have prepared for this day in order to guide people back to a natural, healthy mind and life. In their deep, universal, spiritual faith, known today as the Integral Way, there exists a saying: "Heaven is big, Earth is big, and Humans are big, but Nature is the biggest of all." There does not seem to be anything wrong with this understanding. Viewed from other faiths, the saying can be reinterpreted as: "God is high, Buddha is high, and Allah is high, but the Mother Universe is the deepest source and power of all images."

As humans need some spiritual establishment to help guide them to live well, we recommend you focus on the Mother Universe, with her natural rhythmic order and cyclic movement, as a model for the health and management of your lives.

She is the new common faith of humanity. Perhaps you experience some subtle resistance to this call. Even if you are able to experience subtle phenomena though, you should understand that the source of all those phenomena comes from your own life, which has been endowed to you by the Mother Universe.

God, Allah, and Buddha are the different moral expressions of an inner, subtle reality endowed by the Mother Universe. The only problem is that inner reality needs your special care. You cannot rely on someone else, or some divine image of your own creation to take care of it for you. God, Allah, Buddha, or whatever name you give to the subtle reality needs your cooperation. Care from the subtle realms of life can happen, but it depends on your own honest work.

Dear brothers and sisters that is the duty of your mind—your bare, natural mind. You may have never seriously applied yourself to the spiritual side of your life, and that is what is missing. It is your human responsibility. How can anyone ignore the big background of life? Big-hearted people can see that the Mother Universe is a part of their life. Small-hearted people should at least appreciate that the Mother Universe provides them with a playground to exercise their mental capacity to get what they want.

We encourage you to develop faith in the Mother Universe. She is the true reality of life. Although she is too enormous to see, we can observe her working through our individual lives. By observing human life, we can see what is healthy and beneficial to our lives, and what is unhealthy and harmful.

Even though our physical being is limited by aging, the Mother Universe provides each of us with the opportunity to revitalize our lives, provided we look after ourselves and do not harm our life's essence or soul. Our soul carries the potential to relive. The possibility of everlasting life exists if we are able to attune our life to the universal soul—the essence of the physical universe. That is the final conscious position of human life.

Universal consciousness is very different from the idealistic type of human consciousness that creates finite, attractive names and images to fight and die for. By observing how an individual establishes their thoughts, whether subjectively or objectively, you can see the limitations of their consciousness. You need to learn how to use your mind integrally and constructively, since it is an important part of your life. When you allow your mind to become narrow and egotistic in its pride to deny others and survive, you neglect the whole and constructive use of your mind. You also miss the opportunity to connect with the true reality and positively serve your life.

The spiritual truth of the world is to have faith in the Mother Universe. Realistically, when I pray to or rely on some divinity to solve my problems, who or what comes to help? Truthfully, it is the Mother Universe that educates me through all the events and experiences of my personal and public life.

During trouble or sickness, the true power of rescue comes from the Mother Universe via the nature of our bodily life, due to our good discipline, personal development and spiritual self-cultivation. She helps those who help themselves. By learning some meditation and energy conducting exercises such as *dao-in* or *t'ai chi*, we can help ourselves. However, we cannot forget that the central practice is to have faith in the Mother Universe. As humans, we are able to extend our consciousness as far as the Mother Universe, and if we continue to keep company with her our lives will progress even further.

Who among you has gathered the blocks to obstruct and hinder the spiritual progress of humanity? It is not Jesus, Buddha, Mohammed, Mani or any of the other sincere sages. It is you, yourself, who fails to see that spiritually all people and all lives together with the Mother Universe are one huge being and that all the fighting among people, no matter how big or small, is circumstantial.

As the sons and daughters of the Mother Universe, we are equipped with the natural power of consciousness. We have the privilege and potential to explore her vast house and garden, and to inherit the entire universe. In order to be trusted with her life, we need to develop beyond our limited conditioning and dualistic thinking.

From the deep truth, we recommend the Mother Universe to you. We love her as sons love their mother. We describe her as a group of universal spiritual virtues that act like a guide for human life. Faith in the Mother Universe provides the last hope for humanity, which is drowning in the vast galactic ocean and cannot see the shore. The Mother Universe is the ocean and the shore of life, both of which are equally important in our lives. The Mother Universe provides the rudder for the safe voyage of humanity, while the teachings of the Integral Way provide the chart to guide all of us, and our societies, safely on the voyage of life.

PART II

Reset Your Gaze

You do not need to reach far for the spiritual truth.
It resides in your pure heart.
By remaining quiet and receptive, your life can be subtly inspired.
The wonder is in the mind that knows where and on what to focus.

Chapter 9

The Source of All Truth

To help you better appreciate the truth, we have classified the truth into three parts—the highest or absolute truth, the high truth, and the general truth.

The highest truth is unthinkable, indescribable, and inexpressible. It is the absolute truth. It is known by many names. We know it as the Way, Tao, the Mother of the Universe, or the Mother of all Truths. All these titles are names for the one unique and absolute subtle potency of the Universe. The truth at this stage is indistinguishable, and offers no trace to probe. Therefore, all the various presentations may describe the truth, but they are not the highest truth.

The high truth is the truth of all expressed truths. It is based on a deep, objective, and integral view of Nature. It has content that can be described and probed.

Beneath the high truth, or related to it, are different types of mentalities. These fall into the general level of truth. This level is shaped by influences such as emotions, group mentality and the social background, all of which combine to form a mental pattern. Once that pattern is accepted by people it becomes a social custom. In relation to spirituality, the popular conventional religious teachings of Christianity, Catholicism, Buddhism, Hinduism, Taoism, and Islam are examples of six mental styles at the general level of truth.

The general level of truth is not a high level of truth. It is based on emotional preference and the conceptual mind. At this level, partial views are considered whole and relative concepts such as good and evil are considered absolute. Such a level remains a play of the conceptual mind. Mass religious teachings were conceived at a particular time, place and situation, and made to be understandable for the people of those times. Whatever is conceivable and temporary falls into the relative sphere of the general truth.

The best way to uplift someone from the general dualistic levels, where conflict abounds, to the high level of truth where partisan disputes cannot be insisted upon as real, is to offer a universal and objective view over all the differing mental patterns and styles. This is the Integral Way at work.

A genuine spiritual teaching such as the Integral Way, guides you to see beyond your narrow mindedness to the essential, inexpressible truth. With an open, receptive mind, you can develop the power to discern what serves life in lasting ways, and what serves life in only temporary ways.

Certainly, anyone who appreciates the human spiritual potential is encouraged to grow beyond the high truth to enter the highest, indescribable truth of spirituality. The highest truth, however, can be too remote for the general minds of most. This is why we recommend the high truth, which is more easily comprehended than the highest or absolute truth.

The high truth of the Integral Way respects popular religious faiths as one group of the many human creations, but it places them at the external level rather than the deep, integral level of life. The general religions are recognized for their valuable foundation to humanity's growth, and for those positive contributions and healthy spiritual attainments that are closer to the high truth.

You may ask, what is the high truth behind religious spirituality? That which a group believes and thinks determines the level of their spiritual stature and experience, no more and no less. If the wishes and expectations of a religious faith are emotionally natured, whether they are broad or narrow, they still remain at the level of emotion. And, even though those wishes find expression and are experienced, they are permanently distanced from the Reality, or the realization of the Reality.

If the wishes and expectations are spiritual in nature, they are still shaped by the limitation of one's imagination, because what you hold as the truth in the world of your mind shapes the image of your spiritual experience. If your wishes and expectations are illusory, then all that is accomplished is illusion. Accordingly, what you think is what you are. However, do not expect that if you think you are a king you will immediately become one, because thinking is in one category and being an actual king, as a symbol of social power, is in another category. The two are different things. The connection between them is not automatic; there is a lot to be accomplished before becoming a king.

For genuine spiritual progress, a naïve or innocent mind is valued. Then, whatever happens in the moment is the reality that is achieved. Whether you are happy or in pain, that is the reality of what you accomplish in that moment. It cannot be changed. However, life still offers you the potential to grow and do better, provided your mind is not trapped by your thoughts and beliefs.

Most people live within the cage of their thoughts and beliefs, unless they are able to use their thoughts and beliefs selectively, as tools, to work in different situations. This is called using the false to know the true. Doing so marks the difference between a mind that is brain-washed and a mind that has achieved self-mastery.

The teachings of the Way help people achieve self-mastery. They guide you to break out of your self-created cage of narrow thoughts and partial beliefs, and achieve the high self in order to see the high truth, and open the way to the indescribable highest truth.

The purpose of a genuine, spiritual teaching is to guide you directly to the inexpressible truth. It is time to reset your gaze towards the boundless potency of the Mother of the Universe. You can then move forwards to enjoy the universal morality of the Mother, wherein all people are recognized as one family.

Chapter 10

A New Constructive Spiritual Faith
for a New Humanity

Nature is humanity's big partner in life. Early people perceived Nature in two main ways. The more recent and popular perception, which has existed for around 3,000 years, is that Nature is unfathomable, rough, uncertain, and sometimes even frightening. It was from this strong impression of Nature that a sense of authority over life was produced and presented as God.

It was also around this time that men took over the main roles in society from the women. They conceptually and emotionally shaped God as a superman. People began worshipping a fearful, masculine image of God and the power of physical force. The idea that a single "Creator" created the world in seven days was borne. Not only has this become one of the most influential theories in world religion, it has impacted other spheres of consciousness. The theory implies that time and space was created once and for all, limiting further development.

The other perception of Nature originated from the pure, intuitive minds of the immortal pursuers in China's ancient middle land, around 8,000 years ago. They directly perceived that the nature of the universe is like a boundless valley, which is gradually and continuously changing and expanding in cyclical ways. Governed by its own innate subtle laws, the universal substance moves and performs with gentleness, acceptance, harmony, cooperation, and subtle correspondence. The developed ones intuitively understood that the nature of the universe unfolds itself through qualities that are more feminine-natured, rather than masculine-natured.

The developed ones also perceived that the universe grew gradually and continuously in stages and sub-stages, and that time and space is created by each expanding step. This view allows for endless expansion. They recognized that even though they may not have reached all areas of her valley, her normal, rhythmic changes offer humankind, as one of Nature's offspring, a similar opportunity for birth, survival and growth, but over a much shorter time span. In appreciation of her natural cycles and opportunities, the early people called her The Way or Tao.

It was from these early perceptions that a choice of spiritual faiths was produced. The two main ones being the popular conventional faith based on the emotion of an awesome God, and the other the faith in the Mother of the Universe, or motherly source of all creation.

The perception of an awesome God has dominated at least half of the human population over the last 3,000 years. During this time, the quality of life has not been smooth, and sometimes it has been very painful. Though the pain may occasionally come from Nature, it is mostly a result of the faith people hold onto.

Conservatively speaking, the Way began to be discovered around six to eight thousand years ago. I believe its discovery is one of the most important contributions to humanity. Due to its influence, the Chinese culture grew differently than the rest of the world. Unlike the religious cultures of India, or the technological cultures of the West, metaphysics formed the crux of China's development. This lasted until the middle of the twentieth century, when its influence began to decline due to the impact of the cultural revolution, communism, and more recently by a desire to compete with the West.

In ancient China, the developed ones' direct perception of the deep substance, order, and constancy of the movements of the Way, helped shape the orderliness of life and health in their early societies. Mutual help, cooperation and harmonizing with Nature were respected. People understood that they were naturally connected to each other and to the universe. They were all one family with the sky as their father and the Earth as their mother. The early people realized that by attuning to Nature, their lives unfolded fairly and justly without disputes over good and bad.

The Way is not a new faith or new God; it is the plain and subtle recognition of the way of Nature. The Way is not a shallow faith that relates only to your emotions and sentiments; it is derived from a deep spiritual awareness of life. It is not an external belief, and it needs no help from a religious profession, although spiritually Wayfarers appreciate the support that a religious structure can provide to help conduct its teaching service. They also respect that its teachers or devotees need to be supported in regular and healthy ways. That is one reason why this shift to the Way is made with the important understanding that the Way does not compete with the social conventions of any regional faith; it simply presents the Way of a new humanity. Wayfarers feel it is time for a renewed humanity to stand out to end the stupidity and darkness of people's own doing, and ensure humanity's survival.

What follows is the ageless conviction of the Way of healthy human life. It has always existed, but it is expressed in a new way to help those who have been educated differently.

From the uncontaminated, intuitive minds of the developed ones comes the direct perception of the One Great Same Reality, a boundless, Subtle Cosmic *Chi*[1] or Original Energy, in which nothing can be distinguished. The ancients called it Hun Tun or Unsplit Origin. This Subtle Origin, or Mother of the Universe, is the natural reproductive and creative power of the universe. She has no form or shape, but she gives birth to, and supports all forms and all shapes. She is everywhere. She is omnipresent. As she is receptive to all, she is best described as female-natured. From her indistinguishable nothingness came the birth of stars, planets, universes, and all life.

The developed ones went on to further describe two different spheres of the same Reality—the unformed and the formed. These two spheres are also known as the pre-Heaven stage and the post-Heaven stage of the universe respectively. The pre-Heaven stage is the root of all formed lives and things. Spiritual respect should thus be given to the pre-Heaven existence.

Similarly, human life has two stages of the same reality. The non-conceptual, natural or pure mind is equivalent to the pre-Heaven stage, while the conceptual

---

1. *Chi* transcends human conception. It can be understood, on one level, as the basic energy or immaterial substance that comprises all matter and animates all living things, and the functional force that drives all activities and transformations in Nature and the Universe. It includes but is not limited to sound, light, electricity and heat.

or general mind is equivalent to the post-Heaven stage. Spiritual respect should be given to the non-conceptual, natural mind. What this means is that one who argues and fights over mental conceptions should yield to the higher sphere of the non-conceptual unity of human life. People should express harmony, care and love between one another, as everyone is part of the one family of humankind.

In Nature, all lives are treated equally. If you deviate from the universal nature, harm is created. Therefore, no one should try to act differently from Nature. Unfortunately, most people deviate from Nature by their conceptual creations. This has led to untold hostility.

What is most important to the Mother Universe is the subtle, benign substance of life. Bowing to its plain and simple reality through uniting with it is life-enhancing, while diversification of opinions is exhausting. Opinions are much less important, unless they are offered in constructive service of the substance of human life and the universe. With this understanding, you may be willing to unite with the essence, or root of natural life. By doing so your vitality will increase, since you are busy at doing nothing else.

The subtle reality of the Way is benign and constructive at all times. Negative or violent forces are short-lived. They are temporary expressions of sickness within the permanent enduring flow of the universe. Even if the Way appears to behave destructively, she is doing so in order to realize her universal constructivism.

As a child of the Way, your life is endowed with the same subtle potential and constructive nature. If you wish your life to endure, then behave appropriately, or adequately, in all circumstances, and especially in difficult times. Only your pure, constructive mind can commune with Nature's subtle potency and ride safely with her natural flow.

Too many mental frames have clogged up the house of humanity. The spiritual metaphors of the past do not deeply serve human life. It is important to purify your mind so you can directly recognize that the Mother of the Universe is the real source of your life.

For this new human movement, you need to be clear about the following high truths regarding life.

The nature of the universe belongs to the pre-Heaven stage. The original nature of humans also belongs to the pre-Heaven stage, but the general human mind belongs to the post-Heaven stage.

In the pre-Heaven stage, there is no sense of good or bad. In the post-Heaven stage of human life, the sense of good and bad is taught. Nevertheless, everyone has an opportunity to reform the habits they pick up from worldly life, and return to the original, benign nature of the pre-Heaven stage.

The spirit of Nature belongs to the pre-Heaven stage. The spirit of the general mind belongs to the post-Heaven stage. The originality and purity of the pre-Heaven stage of your life should be constantly strengthened and enhanced in order to prevail over the influence from the post-Heaven stage of earthly life.

The spirit of the pre-Heaven stage is absolutely good. The spirit of the post-Heaven stage is in the relative sphere, thus it can be conceived as either good or bad. No one is absolutely bad, though, because the original, natural potential gives everyone the opportunity to change.

Absolute Goodness is equal to the pre-Heaven stage. Badness is equal to the post-Heaven stage, for being bad is circumstantial. The health of your mind should always be placed above the circumstances of your life.

Good is equal to constructivism, while bad is equal to non-constructivism or even destruction.

In the pre-Heaven nature, there is nothing to compare or contrast with, whereas in the post-Heaven nature, there is always contrast and comparison. Without contrast, the sense of good and bad is not provoked. With contrast, there is necessarily a conflict between good and bad. People of a new humanity choose to live with the pre-Heaven nature.

Clearly all people are originally good, but they may become momentarily lost in the conceptual creations of the world. Spiritual self-salvation is possible for anyone who learns to focus on things of permanent value. We encourage you to be open to faith in the Mother Universe. It will help you solve the common problems of global life, and enjoy life's natural harmony.

Chapter 11

What is Tao?

(As Taught to the Yellow Emperor by the "Innocent" or Lady-in-Blue)

When the human mind was not contaminated,
    perfect vision was produced.
Therefore, why make new things?
Dust off those perfectly good items
    that you have ignored in storage.
The stars in the sky remind you
    that religions serve as temporary measures only.
Here is what the perfect vision sees in life and the universe.

There are two spheres in your life that are the same as the life of the universe—
    the indescribable and the describable.
The indescribable and hidden is the Mother of all.
The describable and apparent is the visible growth.

You may think this description is insufficient,
    but more description and emphasis only leads to bias and division.
If you still do not understand, follow your pure heart.
It is waiting to be your guide.

Although you are able to project your desires to experience what is apparent
    and formed, you are unable to project your desires and emotions to bargain
    with the hidden depth.

Both the hidden and apparent come from
    the same Root of Original *Chi* or Energy.
This Root is most subtle and whole.
It is the outlet of all wonders.

From the One and Same *Chi*,
   the subtle *chi* rises to be the Way, and
   the coarse *chi* sinks to become the vessels of form.
The One and Same *Chi* divides itself to become essence and form.
This is how the multiplicity of the world began.

To begin there is One *Chi*.
Gradually, pure and thin, and impure and thick can be distinguished.
With movement, the Cosmic *Chi* shapes images, and
   then gradually forms.
Both the images and the forms, however, are not to stay.

The unwise strive and compete for what is formed and partial.
The wise keep to the subtle and indescribable Root of Wholeness.
Most people fail to see that the hidden is the Mother of all.

The unwise, in their proud struggle to achieve and possess the describable,
   exhaust and sacrifice their life.
They fail to see that their struggles satisfy a mere part of life.
Although their desires and emotions may temporarily be satisfied,
   their subtle life suffers from neglect.
Gradually, considerable damage is made upon the wholeness of life.
The world is full of people who pay big dollars for a mere penny's worth.

The wise know to keep to the inexhaustible Root that is whole,
   where there is nothing about which to describe or boast.
Most other minds are busy with the relative, comparable sphere,
   but understand there is a big sphere of life that lies beyond.
Your mind is the activity of the Substance of life.
Therefore, knowing to keep your mind calm and attentive to
   the Root, helps your life endure.

The deep Root is not deadly quiet,
   as conventional religious teachers imagine.
Ceaselessly constructive and harmonious, the Root supports your life to endure.
Neither struggling with itself or other lives, it brings no exhaustion to life.

The above elucidations of Tao are based on the
    purest perceptions of Nature by clear and highly developed minds.
By sincerely seeking for the constructive direction of life,
    the early developed ones caused a response from the Original *Chi*.

Their pure minds developed from the invisible spiritual sphere of life.
They reached the wisdom that comes from
    the real life experience of Nature's depth.
Only outstanding human minds can reach this wisdom.
It is very different from the imaginary religious creations
    that came from the mixed and emotional minds in a different stage
    of socially competitive life.
Tao, as the most experienced human wisdom, is still valid today.

Why is Tao so important to know?
You need to know what motivates and sustains you,
    and helps you to grow.
The impetus of Nature makes all natural life tick.
It is the deepest essence of your life.
It is self-constructive and non-exhaustive.
It is natural force.
More than that, it is the Subtle Law of itself.
In some sense, Tao is the most respectful Divine Nature.
Learning about it helps you avoid making wasteful mistakes.

Why is Tao so unknown?
Because it is a quality, not a thing.
It becomes clearer when it manifests itself
    through the beauty, truth, and goodness of beings and things.
It becomes clearer when it manifests itself
    as the Suitability in all matters and things.
Tao is what fits perfectly in all situations, beings and things.

Generally, it is understood that the fittest survive,
    but in Tao, life is not the result of winning a competition;
    it is the result of self-improvement.

Therefore, an important interpretation of Tao is
   that it manifests in all lives, things and ordinary situations,
   as the unique quality and goal to fulfill its natural, best condition.
While beings and things have limitations though,
   Tao has none.

Although sages, prophets, and awakened ones
   exhibit the qualities of Tao, and are close to being Divine,
   as human beings they still fall within the limits
   of gender, race and social background,
   whereas Tao is limited by nothing.

When Tao functions, it expresses Universal Morality or Teh.
Teh is the realization of the Substance of Tao.
Universal Morality provides the necessary benign and constructive environment
   to produce and develop all life with equal opportunity and equal freedom.

To realize Universal Morality,
   you need to care for and discipline your life.
You need to live a constructive life both for yourself and other lives.

Tao teaches you to take steady steps in order to reach life's goals.
Steadiness is far healthier than shortcuts and radical approaches.
Tao guides you to know that the Root of your life
   is of prime importance; it is the health of your soul.
Like plants, the health of your Root affects your entire being,
   but most of you focus on the trunk, branches, flowers, and fruit.
You are attracted to pursuits and pleasures on the outside.
What is the use of a tall tree and beautiful flowers,
   if the roots are not well-nourished?

If you really want to understand your life and live peacefully,
   focus on the health of your life's Root, and
   let Nature take care of the rest.

Chapter 12

A New Spiritual Ecology for a New Humanity

道是精微之气.

The Way, or Tao, is the subtle reality of the universe.
In Chinese philosophy, this subtlety is called *chi* or energy.
Chi is the subtle substance between the material and the spiritual,
    coming before the material or the spiritual.
This *chi* is in its own category—a category that produces all other categories.

Herein lies the traditional recognition of the Way,
    which I believe should be the new faith of all spiritually advanced human life.

一.
道是天地根, 幽微不得.

There is something so subtle,
    that it is hardly felt by natural life.
People rarely notice its existence.
Known as the Way, it is the Original Cosmic *Chi*—the Root of the universe.

因其为幽微, 似谓之稀薄,
其实至精妙, 言语不足.

Being so subtle,
    you may get the wrong impression that the Way is weak,
    but it supports the entire universe.
It is the most refined and extensive potency,
    beyond language and imagination.

虽其似气体，似有还似无.
非同一般气，实作万气母.

Since it resembles air at its most ethereal, or even nonexistence,
　　you are not used to noticing its nonpossessive and all-embracing support.
Neither physical nor conceptual,
　　it is the deepest, subtlest reality of the universe,
　　and the unique source of all *chi*.

二.
以身以况道，道在形之先.

Not noticing the Way
　　is similar to the situation in your own life.
Your life is composed of a body, mind, and spirit,
　　and while you know of the existence of the body and mind,
　　you hardly know the spirit.
Yet, your life's functioning depends on its spiritual sphere,
　　which lies behind the activity of your body and mind.

It is a basic fact that in your life there are numerous spiritual units
　　that are further composed of a multitude of tiny spirits.
These tiny spirits make up the subtle reality of your life.
They sustain and operate your life.
Being too tiny, subtle, and extremely active for most of you to recognize,
　　few people know to credit these tiny spiritual particles
　　for the vitality of their life.
Together, the many spirits in your life are called Spirit.
Do not confuse them with the ghost-like beings of your imagination.

The Way, however, is even more subtle than the spirits of your life.
The Way to people is like water is to fish.
You may therefore imagine it is like oxygen,
　　yet oxygen is just one of its products.
Clearly, the Way existed before, and is more fundamental than the formed world,
　　yet the secondary level of form attracts almost the entire attention of
　　the human world.

形上谓之道, 形下谓之器.
人身肉体气, 气已化成形.
由气乃成形, 有形乃生力.
三.
心思也是气, 但在形之后.

That which is beyond form is called the Way.
That which is subsumed below form is the different vessels of form.
The human body is the embodiment of this Original *Chi*,
   which has been given form.
Through the subtle *chi* it takes on form.
Having form it produces physical energy.
To those of good mental vision,
   the subtle and the physical belong to different levels.
Thoughts are also *chi*,
   but produced subsequently to the embodiment of form.

道气更幽微, 原在天地先.
道气是元气, 生天名 生气.

The *Chi* of the Way is more mysterious and subtle,
   originating before Heaven, Sky, Earth, life, and mind.
The Way is the indistinguishable Original *Chi*,
   which gives birth to Heaven and Earth.
Therefore, it is also called the Reproductive *Chi* of the universe.

元气即原气, 乃在化形先.
四.
由天而生地, 由地复生人.

The Reproductive *Chi* is the Original *Chi*,
   existing before transformation into form.
From Heaven, it gives birth to Earth.
From Earth, it likewise generates people.

生生而不息，大德在能生．
持天地人，故又为正气，

Continually giving birth, the Way never ceases.
Its grace is in its ability to produce all.
Its productive, virtuous fulfillment, called "Teh," is respected as God.
God is therefore creative, productive, moral, and virtuous.
Moral means constructive and virtuous means its supports.
As Teh sustains the health of Heaven, Earth, and Humankind,
    it is also known as the Upright or Healthy *Chi*.
The Upright *Chi* is the God self.

三才皆依道，气正道不失．
五．
正气常，生机以存．

All three different realms of Heaven,
Earth, and Humankind rely on the Way.
When the *chi* of your life is normal and healthy,
    your life is in harmony with the Way.
The Upright or Healthy *Chi* is the natural condition of life.
Nature's vitality depends on it.

正气不可，生命可悠．
气旺邪气避，气衰邪气侵．

When your Upright *Chi* is not harmed, your life endures.
When your Upright *Chi* is strong, evil *chi* will flee.
When your Upright *Chi* declines, evil *chi* has a chance to attack.

社会也如此，发展靠正常．
六．
人类能知此，不独形为尊．
人人须尊道，正气勿．

世界所以乱, 正常已搅乱.
须得复正常, 人类始能安.

Social health is similar to individual health in that its
    prosperity depends on the normal condition of life.
Understanding this, you may also understand that form is a mere part of the whole.
If you wish to live a normal and healthy life,
    respect the Way, and do nothing to harm the Upright *Chi* of your life.
The world is in turmoil because life's natural balance has been destroyed.
Only when balance and harmony return, can people live peacefully again.

八.
学道本不, 在能察幽微.
粗巨为易, 幽微知.
能静方能察, 忙里易犯.
循道方步, 乱致迷失.
以人为重, 当思人是我.

It is not hard to learn the Way.
Just develop the capability to observe the subtle sphere of Nature.
Although the tall and big are easily seen,
    the subtle is more obscure.
Quietness and calm support your observation of it,
    whereas restlessness and haste invite mistakes and harm.
Progress is made by following the Way.
Restlessness only causes confusion.
Respect other people by thinking their life is as important as yours.

九.
大道是恒常, 反常是失道.

The Way is ceaseless; it is unendingly reliable.
It is for all to enjoy.
But your subnormal activities take you away from it.

力粗可以，气微不得知，
气在力之先，无气力不聚．
其治在理气，不在使狂暴．
收得元气宝，人可延寿年．

A strong force can be known and felt by many,
   while the subtle *chi* is known by only a few.
Chi must exist before the formation of force.
Straighten your mind in order to best manage your *chi*,
   but do so without insistence or force.
Gently gathering the Original *Chi* will lengthen your life.

十．
一本道德，本是治世方．
当做玄学看，白费古人心．

The wise forerunner of human life, Lao Tzu,
   produced a slim book the *Tao Teh Ching.*[1]
Derived from the ancient, natural science of the *I Ching,*
   it describes the normal and constant procession of a world in peace.
If you try to make his work a mystical puzzle,
   you waste its wise-hearted contribution.

十一．
常人拜上帝，帝是道所生．
上帝是正气，百邪皆消潜．
十二．
正常须培，上帝与人居．
大道是本体，上帝是作用．

---

1. Refer to Hua-Ching Ni's translation and elucidation entitled *The Complete Works of Lao Tzu*, SevenStar Communications, Los Angeles, 1995.

Generally, people worship God.
Yet understand that God is simply the virtuous functioning, or Teh of the Way.
God is the Upright *Chi*, or Healthy *Chi* in human life and society.
God lives in a healthy, balanced individual, and in a healthy, balanced society.
The Great Way is the substance of the entire universe,
   and God is its subtle, virtuous functioning.

西思合，依正不犯邪．
十二．
正常须培．上帝与人居．

Through universal correspondence,
   the deep spiritual visions of both East and West
   can complete one another by converging in perfect concordance.
Following what is upright, keeps evil away.
God lives with those individuals and societies that cultivate health and normality.

正气如破坏，百神不能安．
如果形不存，神亦失所居，
惜身即尊神，礼拜是安心．

If the Upright *Chi* of your life is destroyed,
   the spirits of your life can no longer live in peace.
If the form of your life does not survive,
   the spirits in your life leave too.
Therefore, valuing your physical existence
   is the same as respecting your spiritual existence.
Generally, religious worship serves only to pacify your mind and emotion.

十三．
粗处称之形，称作神．
形神本不分，形住神亦住．

Your coarse and dense physical energy is called form.
Your subtle energy is called spirit.
The two cannot be divided. When the form stays, the spirits stay too.

十四.
道德宇宙主，天地人共仗.
天如无道德，人地不能生.
地如无道德，万物何以长.
人如无道德，世界成坟场.

Universal Morality is the real Lord of life.
Heaven, Earth, and Humankind rely on it.
If Heaven has no morality, Earth and people cannot be born.
If Earth has no morality, nothing can grow.
If people have no morality, the world becomes a graveyard.

十五.
道是天地母，人依天地生.
或谓气之，本为天地髓.

The Way is the Mother of Heaven, Earth, and Humankind.
Humankind depends on Heaven and Earth.
Therefore, you should know that there is a big difference
    between living with spiritual imagination,
    and living with the plain reality of Nature.
No religion can truthfully deny the Way.
Therefore, the Way should be respected.
You can say that the Way is the most refined energy of Nature.
It is the essence of Heaven, Earth, and Humankind.

无形生有形，有形养无形.
有无本相生，形神交相.

The formless gives birth to the formed,
　and the formed supports and nurtures the formless.
Being and non-being give birth to each other.
Form and spirits support each other.

常自修道德，天地悉皆.
世人失迷途，道德是责任.
引导世界人，同乐太平春.
一身兼万教，道德为至尊.

If you constantly cultivate the moral nature of life,
Heaven and Earth will once again support you.
Worldly people have lost their way.
Universal Morality should be the responsibility of all awakened individuals.
The world can enjoy peace,
　when the Way becomes the guide for all.
Different religious teachings can be learned,
　but the Way of Universal Morality should be most respected.
Why? Because the Way cares for and serves humanity equally.
It has no interest in ruling the world. It has no ego.
The service of the Way as Teh or God is universal.

道是宇宙根，道是万物主.
道是性命髓，道是命所本.
修道不在形，修道不在名.
修道不在言，修道不在求.

In summary:

The Way is the Root of the universe.
The Way is the True Lord of all things.
The Way is the Essence and Support of life.
The one who is with the Way does not serve only form.

The one who is with the Way does not mind what it is called.
The one who is with the Way does not rely on words.
The one who is with the Way does not continue to search outside.

易经是其宗，道德是其衍.
生存形式，不变是其.
慎修易道，世情识其殊.
其则不违正，人间少歧路.

The *I Ching* is its master key and the *Tao Teh Ching* its elucidation.
Although lifestyles keep changing,
　　the deep principles of life remain unchanged.
Be prudent in following the path of the *I Ching,*
　　which will take you from a world of differences to the one, deep Truth.
The essential principle is not to oppose what is upright.
This will help you avoid the paths that only limit and confuse.

修道在知，惜身而爱气，
不再事外求，淡淡无所思.
怡怡自安. 道气便来居.

Being frugal, constructive, and effective helps you learn the Way of life.
Valuing and respecting your life's vitality cultivates the Way.
Look no more for external help.
Be light and clear in your thinking.
Through a joyful and steady mind,
　　the *Chi* of the Way enters your life.

老子身证道，留形二百年.
天下宗教，道德经最真.
其余皆糟粕，精华在无欺.
天下人不知，孜孜向外求，
狂心，醉迷岂自知.

Lao Tzu, who verified the Way, sustained his life for around two hundred years.
Of all spiritual works, the *Tao Teh Ching* is the most truthful.
Its essence lies in a lack of self-deception.
However, most people continue to look outside.
You deceive and limit yourselves by ignorantly choosing
    inaccurate religious stories and partial spiritual beliefs.

安生便是道，无求但乐生，
此是长寿方，合道白长生.
天下不太平，责任须当尽，

Living peacefully is in accord with the Way.
You need not rely on anything else.
It is the secret to a long and happy life.
The world is restless.
Living in harmony with the Way helps in the dutiful fulfillment of world peace.
Those who do can enjoy everlasting spiritual life.

立言近百册，勤奋许多年.
眞言巳立教，能止小儿吵.
建庙供塑像，世界任醉迷.
返身自滋，返心自诚明，
眞言只一言，无违乖我生.

There are hundreds of good books,
    which take decades to study.
However, esoteric teachings are mostly for the narrow-minded and immature,
    and temples and statues are mostly for those who misspend their spiritual potency.
Return your mind to your very life,
    and begin to sincerely nurture your life.
True advice can be the length of one short sentence:
Do nothing against the health of your life.
Health includes the health of your mind, body, spirits, finances,
    and the health of your moral personality above all.

后迟明生道，生道在平衡.
年多辛，其中有无知.

True knowledge about life usually comes late in life.
That knowledge is about balancing your life,
 and not focusing on only one part.
Through many years of consistent and effective spiritual training,
 the ignorant can discover enlightenment.

Chapter 13

The Health of Spiritual Vision

The developed ones of ancient times further perceived that within the giant universal flow of Cosmic *Chi* are levels, or qualities of energy. They categorized these natural energy expressions into three main divisions—the pure, the impure, and the mixed. The pure, or most refined, relates to Heaven, or the subtle, invisible, spiritual sphere of energy, which has absolute freedom. The pure also means organic. The impure category relates to the Earth, or the material sphere of energy, which has no freedom. It also means unrefined or inorganic. The mixed category relates to all life, including humankind. This category has less freedom. The invisible, spiritual, pure sphere is respected as the subtle reality.

From this viewpoint, the ultimate goal of Nature is to refine itself from the impure level to the pure. Being in the mixed stage, humans contain both spiritual and material aspects, as well as a growing mind, which contains the high natural energy of consciousness. Of all lives on Earth, our human life has been endowed with the most unique and complete energy. Therefore, we have a natural choice to either refine ourselves to become pure, and attain a free and deathless life, or devolve to be dominated by the heavy and coarse energy of the material side of life. What we choose, and our subsequent destiny, is connected to the purity and clarity of our consciousness.

The perceptions of the developed ones came from their pure and direct observations of natural energy conditions. There was no involvement of good and bad. Duality has no fundamental existence in human nature; it is circumstantial and temporal. Popular religious culture, however, promotes dualism with statements such as: "Do not allow evil to win over good, but allow good to win over evil." Such statements invite competition among people. At worst, they imply that the winner is believed to be good and the loser bad. People believe the winner has God's approval. The belief that "might is right" has become a popular human faith, supporting innumerable unrighteous wars which are symptoms of an unhealthy culture. Should we continue these inappropriate divisions?

Based on the three divisions of the Way, the matter of living a good life is not about winning a competition; it is about self-refinement or self-improvement. The common goal is to live safely among all types of relationships.

Humans rank as equal partners with Heaven and Earth. Together these three spheres comprise the Three Children, or Three Purities of the Mother Universe. Since humans are more than mere animals, the laws that apply to humans should be different from the laws that apply to the jungle. From the ancient humanistic culture and the *I Ching*, we know that the natural duty of people is to improve and strengthen themselves, and live a life of Integral Truth.

Each one of the Three Purities has a *yang*, or pure side, and a *yin*, or impure side. This implies that there is both a normal and subnormal circumstance in each sphere. Absolute perfection is not implied in any sphere of life or things. Therefore, no perfect condition is guaranteed in human life. The early Chinese did not entertain the thought to move to Heaven.

The early Wayfarers understood the term "purity" to mean benign or spiritual health. Therefore the purity of Heaven means the healthy spiritual power of the sky. The purity of the Earth means the healthy spiritual power of the Earth, and the purity of humankind means the healthy spiritual force in human life. They understood that "natural" means the healthy, normal condition of the Three Purities. Therefore, health is the normal condition of things, whereas the circumstantial suffering of people is subnormal.

In the teachings of the Integral Way, God and Satan are not considered equally paired energies. Rather, a healthy Sky, healthy Earth, and healthy Humankind represent the normal, trouble-free condition of things. Impurity suggests a temporary and circumstantial, subnormal situation. The normal and healthy performance of the universe has no equal.

From the early humanistic culture of the Way, I offer the following guidance.

塵世多幻變.

The dusty and unclear world of humanity is full of confusing changes,
    which obscure the perception of the deep reality of life.
The normalcy and constancy of Nature can be relied upon.
Wise are those who respect it in the conduct of their lives.

由三還返一,
惟抱一氣清.
不用強細分.

Human life can be effectively controlled
    by the three big spheres of natural energy,
    all of which come from, and return to the One Unified Root.
The only appropriate practice for you is to embrace Unity.
There is no need to adopt preferences,
    insist on divisions and argue over right and wrong.

居濁不染塵,
一氣尊清微.
抱一以馭萬,
含元樂清淳.

Although the world can be impure, you can detach from it.
Respect the most subtle.
Embrace Unity in order to govern the diversity of worldly things,
    and contain the Origin through joyful purity.

Although China has suffered from internal and external tensions, the early perceptions of its developed ancestors are still the foundation of human nature. Their early humanistic culture is worth re-exploring, since without its objectivity and universality, no one can clearly observe the Truth.

Chapter 14

The Meeting of Spirit with Form

For many eons, the universe was barren. Gradually, tiny, subtle particles or spirits appeared. With numbers as numerous as sand in the ocean, those invisible particles of Nature gathered together to form groups of *chi* and nebulas. They took form whenever conditions were opportune. This was how the first form of life appeared in the universe. Different creatures evolved from the subtle particles, which were shaped and influenced by the different environmental conditions. The formation of life relies on the subtle energy and movement of Nature. Truthfully, Nature, or as traditionally termed, the Way, is the Mother of all.

After a great deal more time and with enormous effort, the formed life of the spirits evolved to a higher sphere with a certain conscious energy. Gradually, through the successful cooperation of the invisible, internal spirits and the evolving external form, humans evolved to be the highest conscious form of life. Looking at the enormous amount of time and effort it has taken for human life to evolve, it is only fitting that we should value and respect our current physical form with its internal spirits.

Nature no longer produces humans directly as we have changed into sexually reproducing beings. Humans are conceived by parents. As individual human beings, we receive both a physical and spiritual transfer from our parents, as well as energies from the Sky or Heavenly Father, and Earth Mother. We also have the ability to sublimate our sexual energy and produce more spirits. Our individual development is influenced by the spiritual inheritance from our parents, and the genetic inheritance passed on from our ancestors. On top of this, continuous spiritual self-cultivation is still a significantly important factor in shaping our personal destiny and fortune. Generally, spiritual development and achievement can begin with the fulfillment of good will via good deeds.

Humanity, as a whole, also carries a spiritual inheritance. Like children from a family, it can do better or worse than its parents, grandparents or ancestors up to seven generations back. Within a race or nation, where people share a common and specific spiritual background, the destiny and fortune of those people is decided by the quality and stature of their spiritual and social leaders.

The formation of life is the natural tendency of the universe. If we view the universe as a random creation, human life is but one product of Nature's accident. However, if we see Nature as developing progressively in stages, evolving better with each stage, then Nature has a purpose.

The universal nature has an upgrading direction. Like a big refinery it keeps looking for better growth and refinement of its products. All life is given the opportunity to better fulfill itself. So, if we wish to enjoy a progressive spiritual life, we should merge with the constructive nature and upgrading purpose of the universe, rather than escape life's obligations through spiritual fantasy and excuses.

Evidence of Nature's upgrading purpose comes from human life. Most people, except those who are overly emotional, desire to live and do better. We only have to look at the strong competition between people to be convinced of that. The desire for a better life is a natural and benign impulse. However most of us, on account of being confused by many cultural establishments, either try to deny this tendency or exaggerate it. So it is difficult for most people to live plainly and honestly.

Whether we live spiritually and morally, or unspiritual and immorally, is a result of how we manage and fulfill that benign impulse to do better. Trouble arises when we use our low, animal nature of emotion and selfish competition to achieve a better life. The world then becomes sick. However, when we act from our higher nature to live cooperatively and morally both for ourselves and for others, constructive progress is made. We can actually merge with the constructive, moral development of the universe, which is God. God, therefore, is a direction to develop; it is not an available force on which to rely.

God presents constructiveness. God presents development. God presents the healthy prosperity of life. God presents the continual improvement and development of life. God is the constructive life spirit of people. God is the spiritual potential of people, whereas a personified God is merely for our mental convenience.

The universal nature has a constructive purpose, and whatever the stage of life, the spirits carry this innate tendency for improvement and refinement. This is how the spirits of life moved through different stages to eventually form human life. It is our hope that the human form, with its internal spirits, can continue to improve. Our spiritual or Godly potential has to be developed from the inside out. This is what enables us to handle troubles, both past and present.

For this purpose, the redirection of our lower, animal impulse towards a broader cooperative and constructive style of relating should be the spiritual mission of both old and new spiritual traditions. This is difficult to fulfill immediately because there are leaders and people who remain at a lower level of mentality, having not yet developed into the fullness of their physical and spiritual functioning.

In this stage of human life, most people suffer from tremendous conceptual blockage and a poor understanding about the deep root of spiritual life. While a constructive education can help to remove some of the blockage, progress would certainly be advanced if religious and social leaders were more open towards a deep understanding and correct pursuit of human spirituality.

Some spiritual cultures encourage people to worship the spirits in their life and disrespect their body. They ignore the fact that the spirits and the physical body are partners, and are tightly united. In other cultures, the desire to preserve the form of life is strong, as evidenced by the building of grandiose structures, such as the Egyptian pyramids and the Chinese emperors' tombs for the remains of those who have passed.

The Integral Way teaches us that our life is a result of a partnership between its physical and spiritual spheres. By supporting their coexistence, and balancing their strengths, we have the chance to realize completeness and be a living truth of the universe. We can be a model of the union of Heaven or God in human form or, in other words, a model of the union of the natural spirits and the human form. Therefore, we are encouraged to shift any lofty thoughts about our form or spirit towards taking care of our whole life. This is necessary if we want to be a part of the constant improvement of life, because in order for us to improve, the spirits and the form of our life need to improve together. It is incorrect and untruthful to disrespect one side of life in favor of the other.

It follows that we are discouraged from being overly physical, such as indulging in carnal pleasure, or being overly spiritual, such as being obsessed with conventional religious fantasy. We are also discouraged from being overly socialistic or overly individualistic. In the former, we tend to ignore individual duty and development, and in the latter we tend to devalue other people and society. A balanced or trouble-free life is the essence of the Way. With balance and correct direction, we and our societies can regain health.

Chapter 15

The Way is the Source of All Faiths

H o w   S h o u l d   W e   L i v e ?

As the offspring of Nature, how should we live? Learning from the Mother Universe we can see that the big life begets all small lives, and takes care of them too. This is the moral spirit we should fulfill in our own lives. Instead, we fight and compete with one another a great deal. Are we following the nature of the universe? She does not fight or compete. We have misconceived and been misled about the nature of life.

Can we appreciate the uniqueness of both the universe and our high conscious potential, and at the same time, manage our earthly nature in order to give up the competitive fight? Is this thought too fanciful?

Harmony is the universal nature of the Way. By following the Way of the big universe, we too can harmoniously fulfill our small lives. Cooperation is our only opportunity to survive.

W h a t   i s   t h e   P o s i t i o n   o f   G o d ?

God is a product of human culture. In a healthy sense, God is the expression of the subtle moral nature of the universe.

To the general minds of the masses, God is presented as a supreme power, commanding over the weak and less powerful. As early people were less confident with natural life, conventional religions relied on a powerful figure in order to control people. Religious promoters shaped God with masculine tendencies, leading to tension and destruction and obscuring the feminine qualities of life. Truthfully, the Mother Universe is kind, gentle, and equally supportive of all lives. Does believing in a dominating power have anything do with morality? Are such beliefs really correct?

Can the Way Be Our Universal Faith?

Being so accustomed to conventional notions of God, you fail to see you have been misinformed. The Way of the universe is constructive and supportive, but rather than see this, you insist on ingrained concepts about God. Can you consider the pure and integral vision of the Way?

In our human lives there are three levels of strength—physical, mental, and spiritual. The physical is the low level; the mental is the middle level, and the spiritual is the high level. War is at the physical level, and the conceptual religious conflicts are at the mental level. The universal moral strength of life is the real spiritual level of life.

The moral standard of the Way is not to harm or fight with anyone. By straightening and simplifying your life, all three levels can work together in harmony with the moral nature of the Way.

The Way is the gentle, moral God behind all lives and all things. Believing in Universal Morality is the only way out of the destructive tendency of the world. It is the safest and most reliable faith for everyone.

The Way and Other Faiths

The Faith of the Way

> The Way is the unique source of the universe.
>
> The Way is its own source.
>
> The Way has no peer.
>
> The Way is everlasting.
>
> The Way is formless.

The Way is all able.

The Way is indivisible.

The Way is all penetrating.

The Way is soundless and colorless.

The Way gives birth to all.

The Way is beyond the descriptive mind; it cannot be defined.

The Way is unnameable, but it is the Mother of all nameable beings and things.

The Way is the source of all faiths.

The Way remains as the moral confidence of all life.

The Way has escaped the notice of general society.

The Faith of Christianity

The Way is the deep spiritual source of Jesus's teaching. Both the Christian God and the Way have been described by similar characteristics. There are three specific words used to describe the Christian view of God that parallel Lao Tzu's description of the Way in the *Tao Teh Ching*.

God is "omnipresent." This is equivalent to the all pervasiveness of the Way. The Way can be left, right and everywhere.

God is "omnipotent." This is equivalent to the concepts of, the greatest wisdom appears foolish, the best craftwork appears clumsy, and the greatest accomplishment looks as if nothing has been accomplished.

God is "omniscient." This is the same as the greatest knowledge is like knowing nothing.

The Faith of Islam

The Way spiritually inspired Mohammed. Allah is described by characteristics that are similar to those of the Way.

Allah is the only One.

Allah is the True Lord creating Heaven, Earth, and all life.

Allah is all knowable.

Allah is all capable.

Allah is eternal.

Allah is able to penetrate all things.

Allah is indivisible substance.

Allah has no beginning and no end.

Allah is formless.

Allah is soundless and colorless.

Allah is beyond any sense of direction.

Allah is the highest God of no specific place.

The Faith of Buddhism

The Way in Buddhism is the spiritual reflection that led to the reformation of the socially suppressive Brahman religion to the more open teachings of Buddhism.

Whatever you call the universal subtle potency, whether it be the Way, God, Allah or Buddha, know that all these titles are names for the absolute spiritual reality. However, for the conceptual level of presentation, I have observed that each faith expresses a spiritual temperament which I have matched to the four seasons of the year. The teaching of the Way is equivalent to spring. The teaching of Jesus is equivalent to summer. The teaching of Mohammed is equivalent to autumn, and the teaching of Sakyamuni is equivalent to winter. However, as we observe with the Way, behind all the changes, the ceaseless rotation of the year remains unchanged.

My   Humble   Reflection

Language is used for the purpose of mental communication. But beyond names and ideas, no knowledge can be presented. This is why the Way is simply presented. Describing the Way as unnamable indicates its absoluteness.

Spiritually, aside from minor differences, the worship of absoluteness by all four faiths is fundamentally the same. Thus, one wonders where all the religious conflict comes from. It arises from social competition, which spoils the harmony within and between spiritual teachings. But isn't peace and harmony among people one of the supposed outcomes offered by spiritual teachings? I hope both the leaders and the believers can give some thought to this and begin to reflect more deeply.

I respect that each faith has presented the spiritual effort of people at different times and in different places, but now there exists the need for their mutual cooperation. It is time to respect the essence of all teachings, and use the minor differences of style for the different seasons and stages of life. The teachings can supplement each other in order to make the different seasons of life turn round.

It is dangerous to sweep away all differences, as human life is organic and grows at different stages. We can use the constructive aspects of the different teachings to serve the different stages of human life. The universal nature of the Way allows for all types of constructive efforts. Naturally, this is the spiritual attitude of the "Path of Constructive Life" (PCL). However, we should not be deceived by the factitious and imaginative wording of religions, which tend to obstruct one's vision of the reality of life and Nature.

Religion can be a temporary support to help you get through troubled and emotional times, when your mind is still immature. However, it should not become your permanent home. It is important to keep evolving beyond the creations of your mind. As a spiritual worship, the Way is the Absolute Spirit of the universe. It is the deep spiritual leadership of humankind. It is the direct spiritual perception and projection of humanity. Let us worship the Spirit of Absoluteness without doubt or dispute.

Chapter 16

The Universal Mother

The Human Mind Develops from Nature;
Nature Does Not Develop from the Mind

The Universal Mother refers to the motherly source of the universe. Faith in the
Universal Mother reflects the reality that the universe is self-creating, in contrast
to the human view that a Great Spirit creates the universe. Faith in the Universal
Mother also reflects the reality that the human mind developed from Nature, in
contrast to any belief that the human mind created Nature.

The Mother of the Universe
    is the source of all beings, nonbeings and all things.
She is the Integral Truth.
She is the inspiration to humanity.

As her child, I am able to reflect upon her Nature,
    and become aware that her Integral Truth is the nature of the universe,
    and the nature of all individual lives.
Addressed as the Way or Tao,
    her integral truth is respected as the non-created Cosmic Being in all entirety.
Its teachings reflect the subtle reality of the universe and all life.

The Way is the Mother of the Universe.
Existing prior to the beginning of time or space, it is unlimited,
    but it gives birth to the limited.
The limited, in turn, supplements the unlimited without end.
This is why the boundless cosmos has become so.

Boundlessness is the nature of the universe.
It is inconceivable by the human mind,
    though the mind tries hard to do so.

These struggles and attempts by the mind are only evidence
    that it knows nothing about the spiritual nature of life and the Universe.
The boundlessness of the Universe has only one nature,
    the constructive nature of the Way.

The Way is the non-created Nature,
    or Subtle Origin of the Universe that brings forth all creation.
Creation is but the non-created Origin revealing itself.
The being that can be known by gender
    is but the offspring of the Non-Gender.
The being that is known and seen by form
    is made so by the Formless.
All spiritual phenomena, such as God, spirits and deities,
    are but the natural spiritual functioning
    of the non-created substance of the Universe.

The beginning and the endless development of the Universe
    is but the natural consequence of Nature's self-activation.
It has nothing to do with the mind,
    though the general mind tries cleverly to think so.

Conceptions are just products of the conscious mind.
The Subtle Reality of Nature is beyond conception.
The Subtle Reality is not a product of some conceptual God,
    and neither is the human mind.

The Divine Plan is Produced
by Natural Impetus

Nature reveals itself through its own manifestations,
    unfolding and transforming via its own Universal Subtle Law.
The Subtle Law is the operation and pattern of Nature
    as recognized by achieved human beings.

The Subtle Law exists right next to us.
Generally, it is undetectable by the general mind,
    however it can be perceived by the highly developed mind.

The Subtle Law is based on cosmic energy correspondence,
    whereby the same energy wavelengths attract each other.
It vibrates at a very low, almost nonexistent frequency.
All life is connected to its network of highly responsive, subtle energy.
Therefore, what is deep within your mind
    causes a corresponding response in the external world.

The developed ones recognized that Nature's self-creative work
    results from the interplay of two polar forces,
    which are continuously seeking balance,
    and continuously ready to turn around.
Thus, natural cyclic patterns constantly form.

All natural movement carries this opportunity for turning around.
Look at the heavenly planets and stars, drawing ceaseless circles in the sky.
Big circles, small circles, vertical circles and horizontal circles,
    all compose the activity of cosmic life.

The cosmos cycles and spirals,
    like an achieved individual performing *t'ai chi*.
Does someone decide that the movement should be cyclic,
    or does an achieved one learn to imitate the life of the cosmos for their exercise?

The power behind the cyclic movement is natural impetus,
    which some have misconceived to be a Giant Spirit.
That could have been due to the limitations of language
    or unsuitable communication.

Nature expresses itself through natural impetus.
This impetus should be recognized as the only force of natural life.
Nondiscriminatory and just so, it is beyond conceptions of good and bad.

The natural impetus is one whole and unified energy expression.
It is comprised of two opposing forces in constant search for balance.
In other words, the One Reality is made up of two different and alternating forces,
    between which there is interdependence and dynamic unity.
Once their movement reaches a critical point, a new balance is required.

The discovery of this natural pattern led to the principle of *yin* and *yang*,
   and the Ultimate Law as represented in the T'ai Chi diagram.

Yin can be loosely described as being more physical, dense and contractive;
   while *yang* is more ethereal or spiritual, light, and expansive.
Not separate, the two continuously move and transform into each other.
There is no absolute or permanent division
   between the physical and spiritual spheres of the Universe.
What is now called physical can transform to be nonphysical.
Names are used simply for human convenience,
   and for discernment of the natural functions.

In normal circumstances,
   this consistent pattern of unity in movement expresses a natural rationality
   in which people could place their trust and confidence.
Though occasionally, in certain conditions,
   it was usual to experience some partial subnormality.

This basic pattern and law is how Nature operates.
It applies equally to all beings and things.
Developed humans observed that the activity of human life
   carries the same basic pattern.
This is how your high conscious mind can recognize Nature.

Knowing about these things inspires you
   to live a good and constructive life,
   because under the law of energy correspondence,
   good or bad fortune depends on your thoughts
   and personal behaviors from moment to moment.
When you think of someone, someone is thinking of you.
When you stir up hate about someone, a similar thought arises in that person.
Good behavior invites blessings, and bad behavior invites troubles.

The deep nature of the Universe
   has its own wisdom beyond the judgment and control of your mind.
Suffering is mostly due to your undeveloped mind,
   which is ignorant about the natural forces and subtle laws.

Knowing that your thinking and behavior has a subtle influence on your life,
  both inwardly and outwardly, needs to be rediscovered.
That is why we recommend the Path of Constructive Life.

Before the Development of Writing, Grammar Did Not Exist

If there is a Divine Nature,
  it is installed within Nature itself.
Nature's subtle substance is the real background of life.
Deeply reflecting on your experiences and external challenges
  leads to the growth of your conscious mind.
Nature helps the development of your high conscious mind.
Do not allow confusion to arise between your ability to perceive
  and your actual perception.
Unfortunately, most people's perceptions are confused
  by their desires and conditioning.
Misconceptions about the beginning of the world arise
  because people are confused about duality.

Duality is not real; it is simply used for human convenience.
Believing in two separate entities such as a creator and creation,
  or God and people, is the result of the confused mind.
The game of naming the creative flow of Nature,
  and making the One Reality as two different things,
  is no more than about six thousand years old.

The ancient discovery of the substance and subtle patterns of Nature
  is really to save the toil of the mind,
  which persists and struggles in its efforts to manage and reshape the world.
The world is subject to the natural pattern,
  and there is not much you or I can do about it,
  except to follow harmoniously along.
There is no special salvation for anyone.
Only those who are ignorant of Nature need saving.

Truthfully, our human life possesses a similar reality to the nature of the universe.
We are a small universe, and carry the potential for everlasting spiritual life.
By respecting this, we have a chance to develop and achieve ourselves.
But remaining confused, we limit the chance to grow.

At least you know for a fact that grammar and rhetoric
   were discovered after the art of writing began.
The rules of grammar and rhetoric are the patterns derived from a group of writings.
So, if you agree that grammar and rhetoric have no separate existence from writing,
   and did not develop before, then you may be able to understand
   that the substance of Nature and the laws of Nature are in fact one.

The Physical Form is Home to Spirits

Observe Universal Nature with its subtle sphere.
Its non-created substance produces both the
   unformed invisible spirits and the formed visible lives.
The spirits do not create the nature of the universe,
   nor do the spirits exist prior to the original substance.
No single spirit can create the form of life, or be a master of your life.

Your body is a big container for countless tiny spirits.
As the tiny partners of your physical life,
   they are the subtle force and foundation of your life.
Being so tiny, they escape your attention.
Your human form can also produce spirits.

Those who believe in a Giant Spirit that created life
   are deceived by their mental creations,
   and miss the objective spiritual reality.
Be aware that believing is a function of the conceptual mind,
   while the tiny spirits function reflectively.

Spirits are very different to anything you have imagined.
The spirits of your imagination are a product of your limited conceptual mind,
   a misconception of the spiritual reality of life.

Though it is true that your vision can, under certain circumstances,
    be affected by the convergence of a group of spirits.
The spirits reflect images in response to your subconscious mind.
But those temporary images have been mistaken for real and solid things.

Some people believe the tiny spirits are human size,
    or the same size as they appear in their dreams and visions.
In reality, the images are particular messages for the individual viewer.
Yet, some individuals mistakenly used their visions, or the visions of others,
    to establish social religious programs
    based on a great authoritative spiritual figure.
This has led to great confusion.

The old personified image of God as a powerful individual
    is suitable for an immature mind in need of an authoritative figure.
Whereas, respect for the reality of Nature's formless Origin
    comes from a mind that has attained growth.

Using the ancient methods,
    I rediscovered the truth about the tiny spirits in my life.
My discovery of their existence is not a new discovery,
    but the confirmation of an ancient one.

Your life is the product of Nature; a small copy of Nature itself.
Your human form can hold numerous spiritual components
    in exactly the same capacity, and operating in the same pattern
    as the nature of the universe.

Once you respect that you carry a similar spiritual reality
    and spiritual order as the Universe,
    you have a chance to attain everlasting spiritual life.
You can know the subtle vibration of the universal nature
    by connecting to your benign nature.
To an achieved individual there is no more obstruction
    between the nature of the universe and his or her individual life.

The Subtle Law of Nature is installed in your life.
It is displayed and executed through the conduct of your life.

Harming your life, or any life, is a violation of Natural Law.
Not harming the spiritual energy of your life is an important principle of spiritual life.
By attuning to the spiritual energy and subtle law,
  which is a mental and spiritual achievement,
  you can know subtle things and receive spiritual messages.
High predictive skill, foresight, geomancy and Chinese medical diagnosis,
  are all based on the subtle law of correspondence.
But you need to avoid being influenced by unhealthy culture,
  as it distorts the original benignity of your mind.
Therefore, clean your mind daily before retreating to rest.

It is untruthful to perceive God and Nature as two separate things.
In Nature, the performer and the stage are one,
  and in your real life, the performer and the stage go together.
When the performer appears, the stage appears at the same time.
The stage can create the performer, and the performer can also create the stage.
In the deep sense of life, the two are in fact one.

Nature and people's lives are not like a theater show.
There were no rehearsals before creation.
Nature is the real rhythmic and cyclical process of self-development.

From this basic fact, the management of your life
  should come from your inner life,
  and through self-development.
It should be based on your pure perception and clear recognition
  of the basic patterns and forces of Nature.
Knowing about these things and your deep natural endowment
  helps you to effectively manage yourself and understand others.
It is far better than believing in a preexisting external authority,
  which does not really exist.
That faith cannot change your destiny at all.

In reality, humankind shares its destiny with Nature.
An accurate perception of Nature will facilitate correct mental and spiritual growth,
  and a positive human destiny.
Personal destiny is related to your personal growth and efforts
  to meet the objectivity in all situations.

Conventional religious faiths reflect the limitations of their followers.
The argument over God or no God is wasteful.
The dispute over one God or many gods is ridiculous.
The only useful thing to do is develop your mind.
You can then grow beyond conceptual reliance,
    conflict and confusion, and reach the deep spiritual functions of your life.
A developed mind is guided by the deep spiritual functions and conscience of its life.
Correctly developing your mind removes the conceptual blockages
    and helps you fulfill your natural spiritual potential.

The deep truth of all faiths is that God and Nature are one.
How do you prove this?
By deeply experiencing Nature, you can see God.
However, from a conceptual faith in God, you cannot see Nature.
This is why religious faith can be a blockage.
For genuine spiritual progress,
    Nature needs to be correctly observed and understood.

God and Nature are one, and God and Life are one.
To someone this statement may seem ignorant;
    while to another it presents an achievement.

No matter whether you are ignorant or truly achieved,
    the Truth is at your side.
Awaiting your achievement,
    the Truth is attained through personal spiritual cultivation and practical success.
It appears through quiet observation and real experience,
    rather than noisy, outer activity.

The Way is Nature

The teachings of the Integral Way present
    the pure spirit of life, and support positive spiritual progress.
By guiding you to move beyond unhealthy spiritual conditioning,
    you can live a progressive spiritual life above restrictive
    religious formality and spiritual misunderstanding.

Correct spiritual learning and cultivation leads
    to the self-discovery and actualization of the Truth.
Cultivating the Way restores your spiritual health,
    and helps you avoid negative contamination.

God means Nature, and Nature means God.
The two are one.
You have one God as the subtle light energy of Nature,
    and many gods which simply represent Nature's abundance.

To describe God or gods as being separate
    or different from Nature is deceptive.
The proof of the spiritual reality of one God, or many gods,
    is a result of your own personal convergence
    of all spiritual reality and spiritual inspiration.
No predominating power forces you to do this.
It comes from your own voluntary and rational efforts
    towards achieving yourself.

Among all natural phenomena, the deepest discovery
    is the unity within and beyond all divergence.
Unity, peace, cooperation, peace, interdependence,
    and coexistence need to be discovered.
These words describe the principle of *yin* and *yang*,
    and the Ultimate Law, which is about finding
    the positive contribution in any new balance.

Yin and *yang* are displayed by the opposition that accomplishes each other,
    the conflict that boosts each other,
    and the contradiction that balances one another.

Where there is possible conflict and opposition,
    there has to be harmony and peace.
When one side is established, the opposite side is established too.
When one side is gone, the opposite side goes too.
These situations coexist.

Natural Unity, Tao, or the Way, is in everything
   when things are healthy and developing naturally.
Trouble appears when health and naturalness are absent.
Destruction occurs when the unhealthiness or unnaturalness accumulate.
Early people understood such a situation
   as "going against the Way," or "going against Nature."

Natural Unity is the True Lord of Life.
When this Unity is not available to the Sky,
   the Sky is chaotic.
When this Unity is not available to the Earth,
   the Earth is corrupted.
When this Unity is not available to human society,
   everything crumbles.
When this Unity is not available to a human being,
   they suffer, and eventually cease to be.

When the Sky embraces Unity, it endures.
When Earth embraces Unity, it is stable.
When Humankind embraces Unity, it prospers.
When a human life embraces Unity, he or she enjoys great health.

Unity or Natural Harmony is the perfect cooperation
   between the two opposing forces of *yin* and *yang*
   as represented in the T'ai Chi.
In both Nature and the human sphere,
Unity is present among opposites when things
   are designed normally with correct purpose.

That which is most suitable or appropriate is the Way.
It misses no opportunity to fit.
When appropriateness is missing it moves away.
Therefore, the Way avoids preference-making, conflict and war.

In all life, what matters the most is the application of natural suitability in everything.
Then there is no need to fight or compete.
An adept of the Way enjoys being and doing what is most suitable in all situations.
That is the Way.

Normality, or the perfect *Chung*, means absolute appropriateness.
It is the underlying support and balance in all life,
   but usually it is not seen or felt by your mind.
Only when it is absent does your mind begin to notice
   the unnatural or special situations,
   or the things of small detail or small benefit.
Among all seemingly opposite situations,
   there is the most respectful Unity and Harmony.
It is the Centermost Way.

The Way is flexible.
Like water, it can move and be in any direction.
It can be any shape—round or square.
It is not a limited rigid faith about Heaven or God.

The Way is in:
The higher and the lower,
The left and the right,
The foreground and the background,
The broad and the narrow,
The edge and the middle,
The active and the inactive,
The clearly seen and the obscure,
The upper and the lower,
The valueless and the valuable,
The cheap and the priceless,
The moving forwards, and the moving backwards,
The coming and the going,
The opening and the closing,
The fully stretched and the shrunken,
The noble and the humble,
The one respected, and the one held in contempt,
The inner and the outer,
The apparent and the hidden,
The moving in one direction, and the moving in the opposite direction,
The gain and the loss,
The existent and the nonexistent,
The soft and the hard,

The weak and the strong,
The good and the evil,
The expansion and the contraction,
And so on.

The Way is the centermost hub among
   all opposing and contradictory relationships.
It is the Divine Nature of the Universe.
What is most needed in Nature, and all creations of humankind, is the Way.
Find it in your living life.

Heaven will not wrong anyone for setting their heart to be right.
No one will wrong themselves for attaining inner harmony.
Outer harmony can also be attained.
The spiritual value of life is everlasting.

The Way of Unity and Harmony is unseen; only troubles are seen.
But seeing the unseen is a high achievement of the mind.
It is a necessary experience along the path of spiritual progress.
The deep nature of Universal Normality should be seen by all.

The Way is the healthy functioning of your conscious mind,
   which cleanses the confusion between the essence and instruments of life.
The instruments or tools should serve the essence, rather than the other way around.
Even a good religion or political ideology is merely a tool for living.
Appreciate the tools, but never sacrifice your life for them.

The Mind is a Tool

The mind is a tool of Nature, and our conceptions are small parts of the tool.
Be discerning so as not to be confused by either the tool or its parts.

Belief is a conception.
Conception is formed from recognition.
Recognition is the result of perception.
Perception is affected by passion.

By being passionless, one can attain clear perception.
Clear perception is the foundation of correct conception.

With correct conception, life can be well-grounded,
   and healthy personalities produced.
Religious teachings were formed before
   their original promoters were spiritually achieved.

From Nature's substance, we receive life and consciousness.
Purely expressed, this natural potency is neutral,
   or more accurately, it is benign and constructive.
We should be grateful to the source of our life.

Nature's subtle potency is connected to our pure conscious energy;
   it is not connected to the general content of our minds.
There is no need to develop this universal subtle potency.
It is almost like air, water or sunlight,
   except that it is an inexhaustible source.
Our general mind that rides on it, however, needs to be developed.

Thinking that our mind and its conscious activity is all-powerful
   blocks us from seeing the natural constructive potency.
Going against its constructive nature, we end up damaging our life,
   although we can never damage the latent universal energy itself.

Only the constructive mind of a mature human life
   can commune with the subtle potency,
   and ride safely within its natural flow.
Respect the natural flow.
Do not twist its simple reality for selfish purposes.

Containing the highest form of conscious energy,
   we humans are able to correct and improve ourselves continuously.
Therefore, if we wish to progress,
   we should follow a universally responsible life
   by living with Universal Unity.

The conscious energy has different levels.
Spiritually, it is nonverbal, and mentally, it is expressive and talkative.
The two coexist in a high human life.
We should not allow the general mind
    to dominate and contaminate the inner reality of our life.

Beyond the level of the general mind,
    the mind can be spirit, and spirit can be the mind.
We cannot separate them.
Unity is the pursuit.
We should, above all, respect the nonverbal
    and indisputable spiritual Unity of humankind.

It is dangerous and unhealthy to use books and conceptual creations
    to suppress the health of the nonverbal substance of life.
The spiritual nature of the universe cannot be presented by words,
    pictures or symbols, since it is unknowable by the general mind.
The inner spirits are the silent spiritual partners of our life.

Use concepts to simply and plainly express
    and communicate the common faith of humankind.
However, understand the conceptual level only supplements;
    it alone cannot unify.
For example, the same story told twice by the same individual
    contains different words each time.
The conceptual effort multiplies.
It does not unify.

Whether you appreciate the deep reality of what I say is a matter of maturity.
Learn to live with contradictions both in your personal and broader universal life.
You do not have to buy what I say.
You have your own teacher installed inside,
    which grows and deepens with every real experience.

The grace bestowed on you by the Way
    is more than that bestowed by your parents.
The Way gave birth to your parents, your ancestors and all life.

It provides all life with an equal opportunity to grow.
We owe the Great Mother our love and respect.

The Way presents all levels of truth,
   the truth of all existence and the truth of all lives.
What is real that must be true; what is unreal must be untrue.
As humans, we should be proud of containing the high potential
   to know and achieve constructively-natured things.

Nature is not hard to understand.
By deeply attending to her, you can perceive the performance of her normal flow.
But with the degradation of the natural mind,
   your intellect has only grown bigger and more judgmental,
   and your heart has grown too small.

The modern intellectual mind interprets everything via the senses.
This information is then sent to your brain, which reproduces images to your mind.
On this, your mind bases its decisions, creates concepts, and stores information.
After many times, back and forth, back and forth,
   your mind begins to trust its secondhand concepts
   and reproductions rather than the natural things as they are.
Two worlds are therefore built;
   the plain one of Nature and the conceptual one of your mind.

Your conceptual mind contains an abundance of flavoring, but little essence.
The truth in modern times is no longer related to the substance;
   it is related to the flavoring and style of delivery.

To directly reach the Essence, the Way guides you to observe things as they are.
There is no need to add anything.
However, being so contaminated by artificial communications,
   you do not bother attending to the real worth.

The modern social establishments created by the mind
   seriously deviate from the constructive nature of life.
Whether culture, religion, or politics, if they are not competing for social power,
   they are manipulating you to accept their views and ideas.

Smartness is exalted at the expense of true wisdom and pure vision.
Are you really sure the world is doing better than before?
Do you have the strength to recognize and value the flavorless reality of life?

Nature is a Flow of Energy

To conceive of a preexisting master who orchestrates creation,
    is to treat the projections of the mind as if they were real.
It is also similar to saying that grammar existed before writing.
Such views place the cart before the horse.

The Way is the way of Universal Nature.
To treat one God and many gods as separate beings
    is a misconception of the mind.
Learning the Way gives you the opportunity to see
    the unity among the diversity, and attain the wisdom of life.

Nature is but a flow of energy that brings forth natural creation.
Nature reveals itself through its creations.
Nature is creative and so is the human mind,
    which is why the mind can erroneously imagine the existence of a mastermind.

The creative flow of Nature follows its own innate Subtle Law.
The Universal Subtle Law is the expression of Nature in action.

The lower forms of life have no other choice,
    but to follow the basic impulses of desire and emotion.
To them, life and death is completely decided by their preinstalled nature.

As a higher life form, you possess an advanced conscious energy
    in addition to the basic impulses of emotion and desire.
Consciousness allows you to observe, reflect, think and imagine.
But you should not use it to think that you are a master of Nature.
By thinking correctly you get helped; thinking incorrectly only leads to harm.
The correct development of your mind can lead you
    to the benign spiritual sphere and universal conscience of your life.

By worshipping pure consciousness, you can attain the wisdom of life.
By living wisely, you can live a healthy and whole life.
You can live a universally moral life.
In this way, the spirits of your life are uplifted.

Worshipping the high level of life will strengthen you
   in order to resist the low sphere of worldly confusion
   where the idolization of gods, social leaders, movie,
   and sports stars occurs.
Idolization leads to social rivalry and hatred.

It is unwise to live with a mixture of authorities.
The wise choose spiritual unity over diversity,
   while the undeveloped allow religious fanatics and fantasy
   to influence and trouble their life, and the lives of others.

Real spiritual achievement is the result
   of accumulating the good merits of a non-biased life.
The practice of the Way is not motivated by self-interest;
   it is about fulfilling the life of the bigger cosmic interest.

It is far better to focus on the benign strength and universal virtue of life,
   rather than live in the zone of comparison,
   which pushes you to engage in endless competition.
The further you move away from your benign nature,
   the further you move away from the support of your high spirits and soul.
Learn to both manage, and be above, the lower sphere
   of desire and emotion as soon as you can.

Unfortunately, most of humanity is still enslaved by their lower nature.
There are a few individuals, however, who use their consciousness
   to deeply reflect on life's experiences,
   and to learn to manage their lower impulses.
They are therefore able to choose whether to
   fulfill or withdraw from the basic impulses of life.
They have learned to respect, rather than worship their lower nature.

When you are able to manage and be above the lower impulses of life,
   you have a choice in the following levels of life.

The first level is made up of the mass human population
   who lack deep reflection.
They function mostly from their senses, desires and emotions.
They live at the mercy of their lower impulses,
   and the influences of their local surroundings and larger society.

The second level contains people
   who select the discipline and beliefs of their life from the popular culture.
Their life depends on the quality and range of cultural choices.
However, most at this level are limited in their ability to make good choices,
   so they depend on political and religious leaders to choose for them.
Thus, they are vulnerable to abuse.

The third level is made up of people
   who have fully developed their faculty of spiritual reflection.
They are able to discern and to refuse the ready-made "clothes" and dogma
   of the mass culture in favor of personal spiritual growth and self-development.
They follow the path of spiritual self-cultivation.
In ancient China, such individuals were the valuable minority
   who pursued and developed their natural potential for spiritual immortality.

The last level is composed of individuals
   who discovered that life is subject to a group of conditions,
   revealing the truth that the success of life can be conditioned.
These individuals recognized that the subconscious
   or spiritual sphere of their life is the center of their being,
   and that their happiness and health can be almost completely worked out
   by correct self-programming.
This level is made up of individuals who have mastered their lives.

Each and every one of you has a natural teacher installed inside.
You just need to clear away your mental contamination
   and follow your benign nature to the Truth.
Current religious teachings can offer a temporary supplement,
   but you should never allow yourself to be confused or deceived by them.

Life is a learning process.
True understanding and appreciation of spiritual life takes a lot of growth.
Do not restrict yourself by insisting on any limiting way,
   but remain an open student of the deep and boundless Truth of life.

Chapter 17

The Cosmic Rescuing Energy

The Purpose of the Universe

Many people see the universe as a vessel without purpose. This is not accurate. The purpose of the universe is to bring forth all lives, both the worthy and the unworthy, and to take care of those lives. This is its unsentimental moral fulfillment. It gives all life the opportunity to evolve. A barren universe is meaningless. Being worthy or unworthy are human concepts, but the Way of the universe discriminates against no one and no thing. That is why the universe is spiritually natured. This is the moral spirit we should fulfill in our life.

The universe is not just empty space; it is an energetic being with differing degrees of thickness and thinness of energy or *chi*. Both visible beings and invisible non-beings come from the one and same Original Cosmic *Chi* or Subtle Origin, whose essence is subtle and indescribable. Divisions into time and space are for human convenience and ease of perception.

Within the boundless, inconceivable nature of the universe are many starry systems, each with a central shining sun. However, not all solar systems are like our solar system with a planet like Earth on which conditions are ideal for producing the high form of human life. As the children of the sun, we have a natural duty to care for our lives, improve our spiritual condition, and help others do the same.

Many people disrespect the Earth. Some think that after wreaking havoc on the Earth, they can simply move to another planet or solar system. Some religions actually encourage people to disrespect their earthly life in the belief that a spiritual paradise lies elsewhere. Spiritually, it is undutiful to disrespect and desert one's home. If the Earth is not perfect, it is because people are not perfect.

Wayfarers recognize that all people are one family, and the Earth is everyone's home. They accept the challenge of being spiritually constructive in all aspects of their lives, and they avoid destroying any life. They love the Earth, and spiritually protect it from mistreatment. Their way in the world is the Path of Constructive Life (PCL), which everyone is welcome to join.

Most people, however, continue to believe they are better off with their artificial creations and thick books, rather than with the impartiality of the Mother Universe. They therefore compete with Nature. In our view, the belief in external religion is a result and a perpetuation of an immature stage of the mind. External religion is generally self-deceptive and in opposition to the original benign Nature of human spirituality. However, in reality, Nature and life are not always beautiful, so what is the benefit of having faith in the Mother Universe?

The energetic potency of Nature is the force of life. It can heal, support, and restore lives. As Nature's offspring, we also have the unique potential of being able to develop our lives, and reach the essential wisdom and truth of Nature, provided we live in harmony with her.

There are many examples of the restorative powers of Nature. For instance, the life of a forest may be wiped out by fire, but after a few decades most of that life is restored. The birds and animals come back. Nature restores itself. Can artificial religious beliefs do the same? As a war refugee in China, I witnessed people's innate healing strength restore them to health without any western medicines. As a child, I observed a friend who suffered an unusual illness after hitting his head on a rock in a pool. Gradually he was restored to health, relying almost entirely on his own inner vitality.

In my own life, after leaving home at the age of sixteen, I learned quickly that Nature is the most trustworthy power. In difficult times, I had very little to rely on except my faith in the Mother Universe, my own decency, and innocence. I explored Nature's invisible power of life, picked up external learning along the way, and achieved spiritual success in the world. Through experience, I learned that the subtle, everlasting strength and universal kindness of Mother Nature is the true miracle worker. Her natural energy can heal and support the longevity of one's life.

Traditionally, the rescuing energy of the Mother Universe is respected as Heavenly Virtue or Teh. Perfectly designed by Nature, it is stored in life. Through the Universal Law of spiritual correspondence, this energy assists you by offering an automatic response in tune with the frequency of your thoughts and behaviors. Therefore, what you think and how you behave is fundamentally important to the type of response you receive. No one should expect the medical system of society to take care of their health. Similarly, no one should expect that their spiritual faith, which in many cases has been imposed on them by their ancestors, can assure their safety and prosperity without their own dutiful attendance to their life. Only those who accept responsibility for their pure soul and good heart, befriend Teh.

People attuned to Nature are calm. They are content with a natural, trouble-free life, and are not greedy for more. The desire for more, including more intellectual knowledge, comes from a place of tension. It lacks the spiritual quality of objectivity. Without objectivity, one is left to rely on external beliefs and knowledge, which in turn block you from objectively viewing Nature, and developing confidence in her ability to solve problems in invisible ways.

Struggle and over-activity only cause further tension and entanglement with problems, which keeps you further away from Nature's subtle power. A well-managed and neutral mind causes a clear and direct corresponding response from the subtle energy. A relaxed, loose and quiet way of life helps you dissolve problems, and touch Nature's subtle power.

Even though Nature's performance appears inactive, it is a thousand times more powerful than tension. The true value of learning about, and harmonizing with Nature's laws is to help you reduce all manner of mistakes in life. Managing your mind and calming your nervous system so that you can commune with the Cosmic *Chi* can be supported by sincerely repeating the following prayer, "Heavenly peace and tranquility are within me."

The worldly style of life always desires to win, whereas Mother Nature's style is quiet and effortless. She follows the undisturbed natural flow of the Essence in all situations. Even in difficult situations, there is always a natural route to find and follow. The attitude of the ancient Chinese is to do whatever is needed with one's best effort, and allow Nature to do the rest. The question becomes how much does one do before turning the matter over to Nature? Sometimes, what you do causes more harm than good. It is then too late for Nature to help. For example, using heavy western medicine like chemotherapy can destroy a patient's vitality before their own natural life force or lighter medical treatments, such as Chinese medicine, are given a chance to work.

Saving yourself and your fellow people is not about doing or creating more. It is about attaining a better and more complete understanding of yourself and the world. For example, if you are sick, it is not about augmenting your health. Rather, it's about removing the trouble through understanding, and allowing your health to naturally restore itself.

The Way recommends deep observation in all circumstances. This requires learning and the growth of wisdom. The work of the Way is about promoting a deep understanding of life with a great public spirit. When a well-guided individual with a balanced personal and public interest does this, God is present in that moment.

Improve   the   Understanding   of   Life

Humans are a unique form of life in the universe. They have been endowed with consciousness. It is valuable for each of us to become aware of our position in relationship to the Mother of the Universe. As her child, each one of us is a small model of the universe, and contains the three spheres—the physical as the Earth, the spiritual as Heaven, and the mental sphere as the intermediary between the two.

Our physical body is the form of your life. Our senses and mind are our life's functions, and the spiritual sphere is the high essence of our life. The high essence is the unformed subtle substance of the universe, which is the Root or Mother of all formed and formless beings and things. It is both a belief and a reality.

Even though all human life contains this subtle cosmic energy, only highly creative individuals know to embrace it within themselves in order to further develop their lives, and reach for the heart of the Mother of the Universe, which is wisdom. Those individuals do not waste their energy in spiritual competition, nor do they compete with the Nature of life. They know the value of living simply and nurturing a universal life, and encouraging others to do the same. They do not waste their precious energy on religious struggle and mental fantasy. This is the essential content of a spiritually constructive life from the Ageless Way.

However, some people are only attracted to the external forms of life such as their physical form, their name, ambitions and material things. But when we value the external forms more highly than life's essential and invisible inner reality, we devalue our life. People who live a Constructive Life, value both the visible and invisible, the formed and unformed equally.

People who do not value their life tend to abuse their life and the lives of others. This is because they have allowed their emotions to overpower them. Emotional indulgence is an inner enemy. It weakens and robs your energy. The true heroes of life are those who are able to see through, and overcome their emotional barriers in life. They never engage in negativity. Consequently, their spirits are able to roam freely in the energy garden of the Mother of the Universe.

The real source of the power you seek is internal, not external. Although the human mind is able to discover and duplicate things from Nature, it is still very far from the Source. All external things and conceptual creations of the mind are a false power.

People who reach for the Heart of the Mother of the Universe are searching for the inner development that unites them with the "Mystical Maiden," or universal wisdom. She is the transparent form of beingness that acts without creating any shadow, in contrast to human figures and their creative activity, which constantly creates shadows. A correct spiritual teaching, like all divine life, should not create shadows.

Throughout generations, there have been individuals who intuitively came to know of the existence of the "Mystical Maiden." She has been valued and pursued in different generations, under different names and images. Her wonderful beingness is the direct result of the enlightenment from the Mother of the Universe.

The Mother Universe is the physical form of the Mother of the Universe. We love the Mother Universe like a child respects and appreciates its mother, and we follow the Mother of the Universe spiritually.

Spiritual Energy

Although spiritual energy is formless, it is formable. It can be formed by Nature or by our life. It is also important to know that spiritually, the invisible non-self is the real self of life, and the self, or what we see and think of as the self, is just a function of our mind. A volatile mind always identifies itself as the self of life, but in doing so it frequently betrays its own life.

Be careful. Watch out for those thoughts that steal from and betray your life's vitality, and befriend those thoughts that are positive and life-enhancing. What you identify as the self can be but a momentary thought reflected out from the non-self. Since the Way values spiritual integrality, where everything is a part of the whole, you should not insist on any distinctions between the self and non-self, though there is certainly room for spiritual awareness. It is not safe to insist on any distinction, because of your limited experience of life. In spiritual learning, do not mark treasures with moving clouds, and then go back to search where you buried them.

Another fact is that theology and demonology are the conceptual products of a conditioned mind that has lost touch with its benign Nature. The different stories and experiences produced by the mind, and accepted as the external truth, are mere reflections of the mind in different circumstances. Above all experiences, the most valuable are an uncontaminated mind and a clean soul.

The greatest truth about the spiritual world is that nature spirits are benign. Their response, whether friendly or hostile, is dependant on the content of your mind. This may come as a surprise to the inexperienced mind.

The spirits in your formed life can live eternally. When healthy, they are capable of forming and deforming according to the need of the circumstance. The high spirits in Nature, and in an achieved life, can form and deform instantly in the right moment and in response to a person of their choice.

The wonderful phenomena of the universal spiritual reality, and the miraculous performances of the high spirits, are usually beyond people's level of experience, and generally go unnoticed. The high subtle beings offer their help freely, although they are particularly responsive to people of a constructive nature.

Although high beings can appear as formed lives to the healthy vision of people, the fact in the spiritual sphere is "one is all and all is one." There is no real separate existence. This fact is not realized by popular religious teachers and people of partial vision. The correct way to view spiritual phenomena is to understand the message that is being conveyed. Do not let yourself be deceived by details of form, color, smell or density, as these things come mostly from your own mental conditioning and creativity. Be aware, though, that there are differences in the strength or weakness, and high or low nature of the message and its source. It is foolish to believe that your visions are real and solid.

Cosmic *Chi* is behind all universal existence. It can help you penetrate through the heavy mist of your conceptual mind. It provides support and healing at all levels of your worldly life, and it is freely flowing and active among those who live a constructive, sincere and pious life. When the time is ripe, you have to remove the dusty, hard shell of your form in order to return to the universal essence of the Mother Universe, where suffering does not exist.

Is Cosmic Energy God?

God is a creation of the human mind, which personifies all the natural spirits of life as one huge invisible being on which people can emotionally rely during uncertain times. However, the idea of God as a spiritual being can also be described as a temporary formation of cosmic energy, or gathering of nature spirits in response to a mental request.

The intellectual question whether God exists or not reflects the personal development of the questioner, who uses a material standard to assess the spiritual sphere of life. This is similar to telling someone that you love them as deeply as the ocean, and they ask whether that is in pounds or tons? The two are totally unrelated. The insistence on atheism and/or theism expresses an ignorance of the spiritual nature of life. The former ignores the internal reality of life, and the latter mistakes the internal reality to be the external reality.

Why is There Such a Thing
as Cosmic Rescuing Energy?

In the sky there is no emergency rescue service to call upon, although people project the idea of God to fill this role. The truth is that people can sometimes cause a cosmic response based on the law of correspondence, by their sincere search for a constructive direction in life. As the energetic support is given freely and invisibly, some people know its responses as help from Heaven or help from angels.

In times of trouble, the rescuing energy is requested spiritually, and it responds spiritually without the need for formality or thanks. Any positive physical result or positive physical change in the circumstances is a coincidence. Unfortunately, what eventually happens is that as matters become less desperate, people begin to think, ungratefully, that the change was achieved by them alone. If you wish to enjoy a supportive relationship with the Cosmic Energy, you should not only watch your behavior, but also your thoughts, as these both invite a corresponding response from the Mother Universe.

Among worldly spiritual cultures, there are two incorrect attitudes that have developed about nature spirits.

The first is that people commonly believe that nature spirits are formed like humans. This is incorrect. Personification is the result of the creative mind. The tiny spirits can, however, affect the mind of an individual, such as a medium, in order to communicate.

The second is that people believe the spirits are troublesome. Thus, followers of primitive spiritualist practices paint menacing faces, and use rough and noisy activities to threaten the spirits away. They brandish knives and spears, and use cold water and fire techniques in the belief that those practices will exorcise the spirits. However, it isn't the practices that really achieve peace, it is the effect that the participants have on the situation when they eventually tire and quiet down from all the activity.

Conventional religious teachers organized their own activities consisting of offerings, prayer, and complicated rituals in the hope of appeasing the spirits. Such activities are expressions from minds that were struggling during times of difficulty and darkness, and which had little or no knowledge about the spirits as the basic foundation of life.

Both these primitive and religious activities are groundless, and are indicative of people's low spiritual knowledge. In truth, it is not the spirits that are troublesome, rather it is your ignorant mind and improper way of living.

As a way of correcting these misunderstandings, we suggest the following ways of living. Fundamentally, our advice is to live a constructive life.

Live with the Way. When you live with the Way, you enjoy a sound mind, physical well-being, and a healthy spirit. You thoroughly enjoy your life being. There is no need for any fantasy. You are in spiritual harmony with the Way of the Mother Universe.

Respect your healthy benign nature. Generally, trouble and suffering are a result of being overly or negatively creative, straining for recognition or for more than what is really necessary or seeking enjoyment through materialism. All of these things go against the benign nature of your life, and whatever goes against your nature, goes against the love of the Mother of the Universe. People who live a constructive life do not create unhealthy living conditions for themselves or others.

Be content with a simple life. Modern life, with its modern creations, is abusive in the way that it tempts you to seek more than what you really need to enjoy life. What is civilized about developing more and more weapons of destruction? A spiritually constructive life suggests you avail yourself of opportunities as they come, but that you do not struggle or compete for what is not yours.

Respect the deep laws of life. The cosmic rescuing energy is continually available to those who sincerely respect the nature of life. However, it has difficulty reaching those whose egos are overly strong, and whose minds are blocked by conceptions. It also cannot reach those who ignore the health of their life and soul by constantly searching for more. If you do not do anything to help yourself, no amount of religious ceremony, prayer, or ritual can help.

Be responsible. The important principles of a spiritually constructive life are a health-centered life with regular, constructive spiritual learning and cultivation. These activities support the health and harmony of your body, mind and spirits, by strengthening their natural potency. You do not need to rely on any conventional religious services. Troubles arise as a result of people's lack of self-reliance and self-responsibility. Each person has a personal spiritual duty to understand and improve their life, and that duty should not be assigned to anyone else.

Love your life. Love your life as the Mother of the Universe loves your life. Your life is no less than any other person's life including those people who wear holy robes. Your life is holy, your mother is holy, your father is holy, your spouse is holy, your children are holy, your work is holy and your home is holy. Everyone is holy provided they respect and take care of their life.

Chapter 18

Faith in the Deep Life Force of Nature

由信致强堪为道

A good confidence in Nature can strengthen your life and mind,
  whereas a general conceptual faith,
  if based on partiality and untruth,
  can tie up and constrict your mind.
What you adopt with your mind is limited to
  your ability to filter and select the truth.
However, if your spiritual or religious faith is based on
  the plain Truth, it can serve to strengthen your life,
  since rewards in life correspond to the mental condition you set.

Confidence that grows from the real experience of
  deep Nature can be stronger and more truthful
  than a general conceptual faith.
When you live in harmony with Nature,
  you become closer to her, and receive more support.

Nature has both an internal and external side.
Most of you are familiar with the ceaseless rotation of the seasons,
  which is Nature's external side.
The inner condition of your life is Nature's internal side.
It can be affected by Nature's external side, as well as by your own activities.

A clear recognition of life is far more realistic and valuable
  than living an artificial one.
Who can deny that life comes from and is sustained by Nature's life force?
Human life is the transformed life force or *chi* of Nature.
Those who understand this and live wisely,
  can beneficially change the conditions of human life.

由信能致强，
如察内心.
信者依外力，
其心不平.

The general social culture encourages your emotional faith
    when relying on Heaven's or the Sky's support.
This is more out of fear than from an intent to work
    harmoniously with Nature for better health,
    mentally, emotionally, and physically.
Above all, a truthful attitude shows your respect for Nature's support.
While it is obvious that good confidence can strengthen your life,
    when combined with your own reflection and self-inspection,
    your life becomes even stronger and more truthful.
Faith in a power other than life itself, can lead to an
    unbalanced situation, and bring harm to you and other lives.

若求心平静，
先须心无欲.
心欲乃是气，
气是身之力.

If you want peace of mind,
    less desire is beneficial.
Desire is an expression of *chi* in life.
Chi is the energy or force of life.

我之能有心，
不为心所苦.
我之能有气，
不为气所逼.

Your life has a mind,
    but you should not be burdened by it.

Life has *chi*,
  but it is important that you learn not to be pushed by it.

我之能有欲，
我生有可．
但畜心气欲，
三力生之宝．

Having desire is something to celebrate,
  but do not overdo it.
Learn to respect and store your pure mind, *chi*, and essence,
  as they are the Three Treasures of life, which together,
  can strengthen your life.

当知珍三宝，
定名为三珍．
三珍本从火．
火从水中生．

It is necessary to value and care for these Treasures.
They come from the fire, or vigor, of your life.
The fire, in turn, comes from your life's water or reproductive force.

能知调水火，
治生之要事．
火不使内燃，
水不使生波．

In governing your life, attune the water and the fire,
  so the fire does not over burn, and the water does not flood.

也乐此水,
光还照巳,
但抱平静心,
水火相拥抱.

When you are at peace with life,
   the fire and water harmonize themselves,
   and the pleasant light from the water shines upon your life.

水火原在内,
太极主和,
身心能和,
人是活太.

Water and fire are your life's inner forces.
The T'ai Chi symbol illustrates the harmony between the two.
A harmonized body and mind is a living T'ai Chi.

内有心气平,
外则无所需.
人到无求境,
天地与人平.

Internally you have peace of mind,
   and externally you require nothing more.
Having reached a place of contentment,
   Heaven, Earth, and Humankind are equally balanced.

三珍何所根?
所根在道气.
道气最养人,
可自败身?

What is the root of the Three Treasures?
The *Chi* of Life is their root and greatest support.
Why wouldn't you value and care for it?

可乐在有生，
生乐不可易.
身等日月星，
友朋相.

Happiness comes from your life itself.
Nothing can be exchanged for it.
Your life is equal to the sun, moon, and stars.
They are loving friends.

人生何可持，
所持在道气.
稍察火起，
汲舌下泉.

What else can your life rely on?
The *Chi* of Life is the most reliable.
When the fire or emotional restlessness rises up,
  exhale and swallow the saliva that has gathered under your tongue.

心泉频添燕，
身火自下降，
呼气方噎气，
水火乃自交.

By frequently swallowing the fountain from your mind,
  the fire will descend, and the fire and water will balance themselves.

不是靠外力,
但凭调水火.
外力善我生,
内力在善己.

Inner self-attunement is more important than external dependence.
While external things may improve your living,
   the inner life force is your real support.

道气是总根,
外内可互辅.
外信加内修,
道氣最剛堅.

The *Chi* of Life is the root of all lives.
When you have an external faith in the *Chi* of Life,
   and you internally cultivate, the *chi* of your life becomes very strong.
This is because the inner and outer forces help one another mutually.

至大而至剛,
沛然莫能禦.
其行仁與義,
道君德为臣.

The *Chi* of Life is very powerful,
   nothing can stop, resist, or refuse it.
When it transforms into behavior,
   kindness and righteousness is expressed.
In life, the Way is the King, and Virtue is its Minister.

明以道作理,
有德是气.

君臣不可乖,
理气自相合.

The Way, or Tao, can manifest as the different Reason and Law
  (or in Chinese pinyin, "Li") in different situations.
Virtue or Teh is the *chi*.
When there is order between the King and the Minister,
  the Law and the *chi* are automatically aligned.

氣以从理.
履德合理气.
千秋與萬世.
亘古不能移.

The *chi* is governed by the Law,
  and through virtuous fulfillment,
    the *chi* and the Law harmoniously unite.
Throughout all time, this truth remains unchanged.

道氣能長存,
致人於不.
道德既不坏,
气亦偕道存.

The *Chi* of Life is everlasting,
  and the power of virtue is incorruptible.
They are two parts of the same thing.
Uniting *Chi* with virtue helps you become immortal.

修氣老益壯,
先例有太公.
光前裕後者,
以老子是.

Cultivating life's *chi* makes you stronger as you get older.
Lao Tzu and Senior Chien are two examples.

孟子主養志,
逆流敢与抗.
后来 張道陵,
立法以求寿.

Menfucius set his life on strengthening his will
    by pursuing life's good cause.
He was thus able to fight the unrighteous headwind of his time.
Later on, Zhang, Tao-Ling strengthened and prolonged his life
    by his own *chi* practice, in tune with Nature's deep force.

華山老處士
生貴此氣.
輔世雖不忘,
却去山中住.

The senior hermit on Hua Mountain,
    spent his life nurturing *chi,*
    and although he lived in the remote mountains,
    he was able to help the world through his detachment.

先輩皆修氣,
裕氣便近仙.
人如信神佛,
不如直養氣.

The wise individuals of early times cultivated the *Chi* of Life.
A life containing balanced, healthy *chi* is the life of an immortal.
Mere confidence in God or Buddha is not as direct
    as nurturing your life's energy or *chi.*

神佛氣之象.
象是气流.
凡流执表面.
崇信但在表.

God and Buddha are just symbols for something that lies deep within.
The symbols and the activity of *chi* lie more on life's surface.
Insisting and remaining on the surface of things
   keeps you removed from the deep Truth of life.

明士直達道,
精純无旁.
氣淨乃屬神,
氣清便是天.

Clear-minded people work directly with Nature's life force.
They do not allow conceptual creations or
   their emotions to distract them from real life.
Pure *Chi* is the same as the Truth of God or Heaven.

正气能祛邪,
和气生可達.
元气以为根,
生气以为用.

Righteous *Chi* can dispel vicious *chi*.
Harmonious *Chi* can help life prosper.
Original *Chi* is the root of all.
Realize that your life depends on *chi*.
Your life is a manifestation of *chi*.

气恶因有欲，
不遂生怨.
氣不可傷，
但在平心气.

Unfulfilled desires can lead to harmful emotional *chi* and unhappiness.
By pacifying your emotions, you can protect your life's *chi*.

心气岂易平，
在水火交.
法从自然，
自然祗是气.

Balancing your inner condition is not an easy matter.
Achieve it by inwardly attuning the fire of your emotion
    and the water of your reproductive force.
Learn from Nature's management, as Nature is but attuned *chi*.

修行高不高，
从信或从修.
信修须兼行，
行蹟可知眞.

Some people believe in the *Chi* of Life, and some cultivate the *Chi* of Life.
Having both—a clear recognition of the background of life,
    while continually cultivating your *chi*—is better.

修練生信心，
步罡与冠星.
天人相交和，
一氣便成眞.

Spiritual training can help nurture confidence in natural life.
Working with the stars and constellations,
　　encourages you to unite your life with Heaven or the Sky.
This is how you can achieve yourself naturally.

法爲信心設,
氣堪入水火.
此表氣之強,
堅壯皆自然.

Good spiritual programs build confidence in natural life.
The strength of your life comes from Nature.
When the *chi* of your life becomes pure and strong,
　　you are able to manage any situation.

氣能通自然,
道通德亦然,
統制自然者,
一气而無隔.

Harmonizing your *chi* with the deep *Chi* of Nature
　　allows you to communicate easily with Nature.
The Way then has the cooperation of Teh.

入水与火,
内心俱無懼.
此際氣心合,
心神一體真.

With strong *chi*, there is no more fear,
　　even in challenging situations.
Your pure *chi* and general mind have harmonized.
Your pure conscious mind and your emotional mind have achieved great unity.

以心而統氣，
一統而致強．
所以能康健，
是故能久壽．

Using your pure mind to govern your life's *chi* will strengthen your life.
Good health and a long life is the result.

自然合自然，
由乎志之．
耶穌志豪迈，
洞宾心坚强．

Uniting your inner nature with the outer one
   depends on a strong will and unfailing determination.
For example, Jesus's will was strong,
   and the heart of Master Lu, Tung Ping was sturdy.

信仙能成實，
無爲是惜氣．
出自修與練，
果實自家嘗．

The conventional term of *shien* or immortal,
   is the ideological address for "the people in the mountains."
These individuals live with complete health,
   and they avoid burdening their lives.
They heed *Wu Wei*, which is about not creating burdens in life.
It is about valuing one's *chi*.
Achievement comes from working hard
   through self-discipline and self-refinement.
This is how a *shien* personally nurtures the fruits of life.
What concerns you is how to achieve this in modern times.

仙家多豪志,
人杰而性豪.
耶穌多豪語,
洞賓詩惊俗.

Shiens are completely healthy individuals with big hearts,
   unusual personalities, and the broadest of minds.
For instance, Jesus made many bold statements for his time,
   and Master Lu's poetry can be startling for the ordinary mind.

皆因修氣壯,
因心形乎气.
當抱道之氣,
清浊定正偏.

The reason these individuals can be so strong is
   because they have nurtured the best condition of their *chi*
   from which their minds find direct expression.
Your healthy, righteous life, or unhealthy life can be known
   by the purity or impurity of your *chi*.
It is best to embrace the *Chi* of the Way.

太白有豪情,
恐是酒氣.
豪情应有別,
濫言焉足!

The poet Li showed grand valor in life.
But his courage was borne from wine.
The valor that comes from emotion is very different from
   the valor that comes from living a deep spiritual life.

形似神不同,
所恃溢乎表.
心坚是仙家,
不退是氣堅.

Although the expressions of courage and determination can be similar,
　　their backgrounds are very different.
Strong emotion can be excited by something external,
　　whereas an undefeatable spirit comes from one's fortified soul.

富貴不足移,
威武岂能屈,
窮达不能,
修氣得正果.

Such spiritual determination cannot be affected by wealth or nobility.
It cannot be bent by force or threat,
　　nor changed by prosperity or predicament.
It is the rightful fruit from a well-nurtured and healthy life tree.

天能降大任,
斯人其是誰?
降志天授命.
大任是天命.

The tasks of Heaven are big and carry no immediate rewards.
Who is able to be entrusted with such tasks?
Only those who can resist and refine the coarseness of life
　　will be assigned a task from Heaven.

大任不是禄,
代天去化育.

天雖不可見,
其因天是氣.

A great assignment of Heaven is not a reward.
It is a task you fulfill on behalf of the Way
    by educating people about the Heavenly Way.
People should know that God cannot be seen,
    because Heaven is *chi*.

担当天正气,
不屈不争攘.
斯人吾不疑,
舍我其谁哉?

Accept the assignment of Heaven and be the Righteous *Chi*,
    so as not to compete with anything nor bend your life to coarseness.
I have no doubt this person can be you.
If this is not you, who else can it be?

人之任道者,
当须苦心志,
无妨勞筋骨,
不懼餓膚體,

Those who accept the duty of the Way
    encounter more challenges in life.
They do not mind hard work and they enjoy less food.

無憚貧乏身,
是乃助练志.
苦其心志者,
專志益不移.

They accept physical hardship
   in order to strengthen their will.
Through hardships and tests, their lives become strong.

天是氣之清,
地是氣之正,
人是氣之和.
和者合天地.

The Pure *Chi* is Heaven or Sky.
The Productive *Chi* is Earth.
The Harmonious *Chi* should be all people.
You each have a natural duty to live in a way
   that harmonizes Heaven and Earth.

其筋骨者,
導引而不輟.
其膚體者,
休糧以自療.

You can help achieve harmony through *chi* movement practices such as *dao-in*.
These practices nurture your body's health.
Attuning your inner life, together with appropriate fasting is also helpful.

貧乏其人者,
守儉知濟身.
持氣之四綱,
修之饒益多.

Furthermore, do not indulge in spending,
   as being frugal is helpful to yourself and others.
These four things of moving the body, internal attunement,
   appropriate fasting, and effectiveness in all aspects of life
   are most beneficial.

This is not like conventional religious advice.

It is the natural science of life that developed over a long period of time, by individuals who lived and explored the Way of Natural Life.

PART III

Communing with Nature

When we rediscover the usefulness of
a natural life, we shall again learn to love Nature.
We shall also learn that it is dangerous to violate our
own nature, the subtle level of the natural order,
and the natural environment.

Chapter 19

Recognizing the Winter Solstice is Spiritual Progress

The recognition of the Winter Solstice as the beginning of a new solar cycle marked a significant shift in human consciousness. When humans lifted their heads to the sky and recognized the natural movements of Nature, they received the dignity of life. Although it had taken a long time for the human mind to be able to comprehend the objective reality of Nature and how it affected human life, this new level of self-recognition and spiritual dignity was soon followed by a tendency towards introverted beliefs that deviated from the plain and simple truth of Nature. These numerous subjective projections disrupted the integral unity of human life and Nature, and planted the seeds that would eventually become social religions. This process of deviation inevitably resulted in conflict between individuals and groups who conceived the same natural reality differently.

Divergent views and opinions about natural phenomena could be attributed to the effects of different climates and geographies. For instance, the seasons in the northern and southern hemispheres occur at opposite times in the solar cycle, even though all people live under the same sky. Recognizing changes in the weather was the first phenomenon to stimulate the development of the human mind to observe and acknowledge a common reality. Human spiritual development is closely related to the recognition that the sky remains the same for everyone, no matter what changes take place in it. This also led to the belief that whatever is behind the sky determines one's fortune. What people neglected to understand, however, were the immediate effects their local environment had on their lifestyles and spiritual expressions. Yet, despite the variations in sunlight, moonlight, planets, wind, water, soil and local weather patterns that occur everywhere on Earth, everyone still lives under the same sky, and shares the same sun. Therefore, we should all remain open to Nature as a whole, rather than become stuck in subjectively limited conclusions about personal lifestyles and spiritual expressions. The natural unity of humankind is the reality of God or Mother Nature. It is far more realistic to accept one another and move beyond superficial and minor differences of style, rather than insist on limited points of view that deny the universal nature of the human spirit.

The recognition of the Winter Solstice was the first step in human awareness of the basic unity of life and Nature. It is a good example of how to use your mind correctly via direct perception and passive experience of the plain facts of Nature to gather the objective reality of life. Even if you confuse yourself with subjective beliefs, and allow your mind to stray from the essential truth of unity, that unity still remains as the common ground from which all cultures and spiritual traditions can best serve themselves and one another.

The intention to meet with the objective reality is the best attitude to have in life. All basic and constructive knowledge about living such as the use of fire, shelter and clothing came from the direct comprehension of the objective reality. Thus all useful knowledge, including spiritual knowledge and its related practices, should be based on objective standards rather than groundless subjective projections. While subjective and external levels of spiritual expression can co-exist to serve the different seasons and temperaments of people, they should never be confused with the deep, universal spiritual reality of life.

Our hope is that you will be inspired to recognize the common natural reality and spiritual background of humanity, and use it to renew your spiritual expression and spiritual practice in support of global unity. You will then be valuing the harmonious relationship between Nature and humankind as the basic foundation of life.

Overall, there are four climate changes that are important to the harmonious relationship with Nature and that are basic to the spiritual foundation of life.

> *Winter Solstice* (December 20 or 21 in the northern hemisphere, and June 20 or 21 in the southern hemisphere)—Enhances the spiritual strength of life, and supports your physical being to endure the period of severe cold.
>
> *Spring Equinox* (March 19 or 20 in the northern hemisphere, and September 20 or 21 in the southern hemisphere)—Promotes gradual growth and smooth development during springtime.
>
> *Summer Solstice* (June 20 or 21 in the northern hemisphere, and December 20 or 21 in the southern hemisphere)—Promotes physical and emotional moderation in order to support the low spiritual sensitivity at summer's "high noon."

Autumnal Equinox (September 22 or 23 in the northern hemisphere, and March 22 or 23 in the southern hemisphere)—Supports important thinking, spiritual reflection and spiritual practice during the inward-looking harvest time.

These major climatic shifts and energy variations are a part of Nature's great metabolic process, which moves continuously in a cyclical, orderly and effortless way. At the duration of each seasonal cycle and before the beginning of the next, a shift of energy occurs whereby new energies are issued forth. These shifts are special times for preparing for the incoming cycle, and for physical and spiritual renewal. People who are aware of this subtle reality live quietly and in harmony with Nature in order to benefit from the energy infusion. They use it to heal and refresh themselves, and to help integrate their mind, body and spirits. By attuning yourself to Nature's cycles, you too can benefit from her rejuvenating and healing life force.

These four days are a product of the spiritual pursuit of the early Wayfarers. It is worthy for us, as beneficiaries of the early developed ones, to observe these days with specific practices. Doing so can awaken the immortal human soul in our lives. On those days, you can meditate by yourself or in a group. You can use the traditional practices of the Integral Way to enhance Nature's work of regeneration, and to help your life prosper and endure. Practices such as *The Ceremony for the Renewal and Enrichment of Body, Mind and Spirit*[1] can help you to refresh your spirit, and learn how to harness the energy of the new cycle. You may also learn some simple, yet very effective movements for physical relaxation to strengthen your body, mind and spirit. For more details of the four periods and their related practices read my work, *The Foundation of a Happy Life*.[2] We call your attention to respect these first, important, natural discoveries by our early ancestors, which show you how deeply related the human soul is to Mother Nature.

It can be more meaningful to observe the natural reality, and celebrate the specific days of the natural cycle, such as the Winter Solstice, rather than a manufactured religious custom or holiday. You can be revitalized and receive healing by

---

1. See page 161 of the *Workbook for the Spiritual Development of All People* by Hua-Ching Ni, SevenStar Communications, 1984.

2. By Hua-Ching Ni, SevenStar Communications, Los Angeles, 1999.

enjoying Nature's cyclic changes as festivals. The Winter Solstice can be enjoyed as the Festival of Wisdom, the Spring Equinox as the Festival of Knowledge, the Summer Solstice as the Festival of Intelligence, and the Autumnal Equinox as the Festival of Enlightenment. Celebrating the first day (or days) of the four seasonal periods is a call for human nature to cohere with the natural seasons of life.

The Winter Solstice is a significant period to observe, as it marks the start of a new solar cycle when the darkness gives way to new light. The dark, wintry conditions symbolize how life (new light) is conceived and nurtured in Nature's hidden depths or "womb." It is an opportune time to reflect on whether you have limited your spiritual development, or upset your spiritual balance by adhering to partial or artificial beliefs and conditions. Through reflection and spiritual self-cultivation, you can release the old patterns and allow in the fresh strength and support of the harmonious new energies.

The Winter Solstice also serves to remind everyone, and especially social leaders, to develop their knowledge from the objective standard of natural reality. The solstice's purpose is to initiate all human knowledge for public service. All real and useful knowledge is coherent with the natural reality and, like the Winter Solstice, is universally applicable. Of course, you may still have subjective beliefs, but it is important to ask yourself whether those beliefs make sound sense to the objective reality of human life. Your subjective creations should not be used to produce perverse teachings that compete with Nature. Thus, while conventional titles such as God, Allah and Buddha can be used as different names for the same deep and natural Reality, they should not be used to support artificial and partial understandings or practices to gather people's trust, as has been done in the past.

When your subjective projections are used in cooperation with the objective experience of the natural reality, new and useful spiritual discoveries and philosophies can be developed. It was through just such cooperation that the early developed ones extended the discovery of the four climatic periods of the solar cycle on Earth to identify four related periods or seasons in a human life. They recognized that winter is equivalent to a time of conception or initiation in Nature's womb, spring is the time to be born anew into the world, summer is a time for the full expression of growth, and autumn is a time to mature and collect the harvest from all the previous stages. It is important to recognize and respect that as children of Nature, you experience similar cycles to her. The natural cycle of birth, growth, old age, death and back to birth again continues whether you like it or not.

From their objective impressions of Nature, the early developed ones wisely extended and applied the facts to shape a theory of the development of the universe. They intuited that the universe, just like a human life, has four stages of conception, birth, growth, and maturity for its renewal. According to their Theory or Philosophy of Development, the life of the universe follows one big cycle that is divided into four divisions—a hidden, dark stage, birth at dawn, the bright light of a prosperous stage, and the inactive, contractive stage when the light fades back to the dark, and a new cycle starts all over again. This theory takes the small yearly cycle of the Earth, and expands it beyond human experience. This vision was eventually recorded in the *I Ching*.

The *I Ching* presents the objective wisdom of humanity. It describes four stages in the complete development of all things as *Yuan, Heng, Li* and *Tsing*. *Yuan* is the original, initiating stage, or inner gathering that occurs in the hidden, dark depths like that of deep winter. *Heng* is the stage of generation, similar to the appearance of new buds in spring. *Li* is the prosperous or blooming stage like that which occurs in summer, and *Tsing* is the stage of withdrawal and contraction like that which occurs in autumn. *Tsing* extends into the early part of the cold winter season where it eventually develops into the extreme expression of *Yuan*, and the cycle repeats itself all over again. These four expressions are also the four spiritual virtues of a developed human life. A completely virtuous individual possesses all four virtues. Such an individual is able to initiate, generate, enjoy full, prosperous growth, and persevere.

In our view, the understanding set forth in the *I Ching* about the development of the universe is a more complete view compared to the factious view that a personalized God created the world, or the modern scholar's segmented view of the "Big Bang" theory of the universe. The *I Ching* is as valid as any new or old social views. But, together, the three views of the beginning of the universe need to supplement each other in order to tell the real life story of the one and the same universe.

The Winter Solstice has been used as an example for this specific discussion. It was discovered by individuals who passively observed and experienced the transition of one solar year to the next. As humanity developed, various individuals observed that the lifetime of a normal earthling resembled the four periods of the yearly solar cycle. Through spiritual vision and intuition, the early earthlings also decided that the universe develops and goes through similar cyclic patterns, since no development follows an imaginary straight line. The Laws of Nature were produced and understood by observing the cyclic reality of the Earth. The natural cyclical changes over a year were expanded to apply to the universe, and contracted to apply to the physical life cycle of a human being. Based on this view, all religious conflicts among people are meaningless.

The early people also decided that the human soul evolves, and that generally the wisdom of a life is not accomplished in one lifetime, since each life is new. Rather, high wisdom comes from the experiences of many lifetimes. But, the fact that one has had past lives is not nearly as amazing as valuing the progress of one's present life. Humans also have the ambition to join their minds and spirits with God or the Mother of the Universe. No one objects to such ambition, although the segmented views of science currently challenge it. Yet, open-minded scientists and the wisdom of the Way can supplement each other to complete this spiritual ambition of humankind.

Throughout the development of humanity we can observe the following three trails—developing knowledge, developing spiritual faiths, and self-reflective thoughts on life. Reflection helps one to go deeper than the former two trails, and can lead to awakening or enlightenment from limiting mental creations. The safe practice is to value and respect all three trails equally in order to make fresh progress and avoid personal or social harm. You should avoid practicing partiality, or associating with confusing thoughts, since mistakes come from an overly emotional and narrow, subjective mind.

Nature is the invisible force behind the enormous variety of life on Earth. It is a life just like any human life, although it is more complete and balanced than any of its smaller offspring. We encourage everyone to return to the basic reality of Nature. It is the natural environment that regulates all lives, not the human mind, although people are ambitious to say and believe so. Our hope is to help you break down the thick walls of artificial, mental beliefs built by the later generations, which seal the human soul within the physical body, and obstruct the original, open ground of human spirituality.

In conclusion, we offer the following spiritual message. All of you are riding on the Earth on a merry-go-round circling the Sun. The moon is riding on a merry-go-round circling the Earth. The Sun takes all his children, including his daughter Earth, to ride on a merry-go-round around the North Star with its beautiful Seven Sister Stars shaped like a dipper. The North Star, along with its starry companions, is riding on a merry-go-round around the Weaving Maiden and so it goes on. There is no need to compete since there is enough room for everyone. However, you do need to be discerning about what you accept from people who come knocking on your door, selling religious insurance for riding on the natural merry-go-round. We advise you to use your mind objectively, and reflect deeply before accepting what people sell.

Chapter 20

Spiritual Cultivation in the Different Seasons and Situations of Life

Each season has both an external affect on your life, as well as an internal influence on your emotions. Everyone is aware of the need to change their clothes in order to adapt to the seasonal changes. However, only a few individuals are aware of the need to adjust their mood and emotion in order to harmonize with the natural cycles of the Earth as it circles around the Sun. These individuals appreciate how emotional health forms the foundation of a healthy and happy life. Without knowing about the importance of self-adjustment, it is easy to lose energy and weaken your life force.

Spring and autumn are the milder seasons, whereas summer and winter are more extreme. In springtime, when the cold weather becomes warm, it is important to nurture an inner atmosphere of warmth and mildness, and harmonize the three spheres of your body, mind and spirit. When the different spheres of your life are in harmony, the energy of your life is strengthened, and you benefit from the fortification of your spiritual energy.

In summer, the heat expands your energy. Although the impulse is to move more rapidly, spiritually-aware individuals appreciate the importance of managing and wisely guiding their impulses, so as not to weaken or exhaust the strength of their life. Thus, they do not overly rejoice or engage in extreme excitement. It is also a good idea not to completely rely on external devices. So, even if an air conditioner is available, use it wisely in order to prevent laziness, or the weakening of your natural strength and adaptability.

People who follow the natural reality of life nurture the sense of life that is above the senses by keeping their minds cool and quiet in order to offset the outer heat. Through this practice of spiritual self-cultivation, you can achieve peace and positive inner growth. As your internal condition transforms and becomes stronger, you will suffer less from the external conditions and diseases caused by the summer heat.

During autumn, most people ignore the need to adjust to the mild changes that occur, so they leave themselves open to sickness. Special care should always be taken during the seasonal transitions. The mild weather of autumn supports the cultivation of a clear and mellow mind and spirit, so it is a good time for reflection and deep thinking. With clarity and calm the True God can be seen. It cannot be seen in a mind that is confused or emotionally disturbed.

In the wintertime, the heat and energy of Mother Earth sinks down from her surface to her core. As you are a part of Nature and experience similar cycles, it is also a time for you to contract your life energy and protect your health. You should not weaken your energy by overly relying on heating devices. Emotionally, it is important to nurture an attitude of gentle joy to soften the cold and dark conditions of the long winter months, when it is easy to become depressed.

Emotions are a reflection of your lives, and your lives are subject to all kinds of change—both good and bad. Spiritual self-cultivation helps you to reduce or avoid the harm that can come from inner and outer negative influences. In all seasons, the most effective spiritual self-cultivation is similar to the practice at wintertime—that of nurturing an inner atmosphere of gentleness and peace with smoothly flowing emotions. The following attitudes exemplify what we mean.

> Nurture calmness inside to offset hurriedness and outer chaos.
>
> Nurture peace and warmth inside to counteract any cold and hostile environmental conditions.
>
> Nurture a smooth and carefree inner being to counteract the rough outer conditions.
>
> Nurture a relaxed and easy-going mood to counteract the pressure from external tension and conflict.
>
> Nurture moderation and patience to counteract jealousy and prejudice.
>
> Nurture a deep sense of happiness when there is sadness or misery.
>
> Nurture unshakable strength during times of depression and disappointment.

Nurture a sense of tirelessness and endurance in order to return after failure.

We encourage everyone to nurture a clear mind and lucid spirit so that you are able to manage yourself in any situation. Through spiritual self-cultivation, you can clear away the confusion that often leads to inappropriate and troublesome reactions. When you face an unfavorable situation, it is best to quietly adjust yourself, and strengthen your life by applying your energy effectively in the circumstances. In this way, you will find the path of light and success. When a bitter cold enters your life, it is the time to open your eyes to see the diamond of your life shining in the darkness. It is the time to turn your life around, and find the usefulness in your mistakes and unhappiness.

Spiritual awareness is the power of being able to clearly see yourself. This power may be called The Goddess of the Hidden Power of Life. She helps you become aware of both inner and outer troubles so that you know when and how to make suitable changes in your life. By maintaining a consistent state of internal balance, you can reduce harm, and difficult circumstances will be less likely to overwhelm you. Reading the following invocation quietly and repetitively can help you find clarity and balance during difficult times.

Mother of Life,
Help me to appreciate all the seasons of my life,
    and know to not prefer any one.
Help me to become deeply aware of the situation that I now face,
    and know that whatever exists,
        no thing can endanger the balance of my being.
And please, grant me the strength of gently flowing joy,
    so that I may counteract unnecessary worry and sadness.
I uphold the Great Commitment of Life
    to not brew any negative feelings within my life,
    nor allow any darkness to possess my being.
Life is joyful. Life is happy.
The Natural Right of Life is endowed to me by the Mother of Life.
The worst sin is the treason of life.
I do not commit this sin, nor do I conspire with
    the emotional thieves of life to undermine the
    greatness of my being.

I do not grant anyone, or myself, the right to strip away
  the natural right of my life being.
No other belief exists above my conviction in the natural power of life.
Using the keenest of awareness,
  I restore my natural right to a good life immediately,
  and I fulfill the purity and completeness of my life.

Chapter 21

Lessons on Life

有一個人，他有四個兒子．
他希望他的兒子能夠學會不要太快對事情下結論，
所以，他依次給他四個孩子一個問題，
要他們分別出去遠方看一顆桃子樹．

There was once a man who owned a big pear orchard.
As the orchard would one day pass to his four sons,
   he wanted them to learn something about the trees
   so they could take care of them.
His sons had grown up in the city and knew nothing about caring for fruit trees.
He therefore sent them on a quest.
To observe and study the trees, each in a different season.

大兒子在冬天前往，二兒子在春天，
三兒子在夏天，小兒子則是在秋天前往．

The first son went in winter, the second in spring,
   the third in summer and the youngest in fall.

當他們都前去也都返家之後，
他把他們一起叫到跟前形容他們所看到的情景，
大兒子說那棵數很醜、枯槁、扭曲．

Once they had completed their quest and returned,
   the father called them together to describe what they
   had seen and learned.
The first son said the trees were ugly, bent, and twisted.

二兒子則説, 不是這樣子,
這棵樹被青青的嫩芽所覆蓋, 充滿了盼望.

The second son disagreed.
He described the trees as covered in green buds and full of promise.

三兒子不同意, 他説樹上花朵綻放, 充滿香氣,
看起來十分美麗, 這美景事他從來不曾見到過的.

The third son disagreed with them both.
He said the trees were laden with beautiful, sweet-smelling blossoms.
He described each tree as the most graceful thing he had ever seen.

小兒子不同意他們三人的説法.
他説樹上結滿了果子, 累累下垂.
充滿了生命果子與豐收.

The last son disagreed with them all.
He said the trees were ripe and drooping with fruit.
They were full of life and were fulfilled.

這個人就對他四個兒子説: 你們都是正確的.
因爲你們四個人是在這棵樹的四個不同季節前往.
並且只看到其中一個季節的風景.

The father explained to his sons that they were all correct,
    but that they had each seen only one season in the life of the trees.

他告訴兒子們不可用一個季節的風景來評斷一棵樹或是一個人,
關於構成一個人是怎樣的一個人的要件, 還有一個人生命的
歡愉、喜樂、愛, 只能在他生命的盡頭時候來做衡量.

He advised them that one cannot judge a tree, a person,
  or one's own life by one season alone.
But the essence of who one is, and the pleasure, joy and love
  that comes from one's life can only be measured at the end of one's life,
  when all the seasons of life have come to an end.

當你在冬天時候就放棄,
你就會錯過你生命春天的盼望、夏天的美麗、秋天的收成.

He went on to say that if you give up during your winter,
  you will miss the promise of your spring,
  the beauty of your summer and the fulfillment of your fall.

不要讓一個季節的痛苦毀掉其他季節的喜樂.
不要因爲一個痛苦的季節就對人生下結論,
持守忍耐度過這段艱難, 美好的日子將在不久之後來到.

Finally, he told them not to let the pain of one season
  destroy the joy of all the rest.
One should not live by one difficult season alone.
By persevering through all the hard times,
  better times are sure to come.

Chapter 22

How to Live Your 120-Year-Old Life

It takes Jupiter 12 of our years on Earth to circle around the sun.
This is how we mark the 12-year cycle.
This was also how the early Chinese marked the cycle of years.
To them, Jupiter was known as the Star of Years.

In a year, there are 12 months.
In a day, there are 12 solar bi-hours.
In a human life, there are naturally 120-years.
Though some people may live longer,
120 years is a natural place to start.

How should you spend your life in that time?
Here are some reminders.

From One to Ten Years

After nine months of hiding in the dark,
  you are finally born into the world.
Time and circumstance prepare you for enjoyment or suffering,
  but it still depends on the spirit of your life whether
  you win or lose at the game of life.

At this time, your mind is like a blank sheet exposed to the surroundings,
  which impress upon it, and which can contaminate your mind and soul.
Your goal is to develop a healthy mind and upright soul, and
  avoid any negative influence.

If you cannot avoid the negativity,
  then how can you use it to help you grow?
Accept it as a challenge, and don't try to escape through religious fantasy.
Constructive progress depends on you, no one else.

If you allow the light from the bright blue sky to encourage you,
    your journey will be a happy one.

Youth is a time to prepare the ground for your happiness in old age.
Wisdom should be your life's pursuit.
Sunday school teachings, cartoons, and computer games
    only establish unhealthy mental and emotional patterns.
These should not be chosen as the nutrition for your young life.

From Eleven to Twenty Years

Although naturally a time for sexual curiosity,
    never allow sex to become your main focus.
Instead, alongside your principal education of reading, writing and so on
    that your parents set for you, develop your own constructive hobbies.
Although your parents should not establish all of your learning,
    it is wise to seek their understanding when choosing a hobby.
Some may prove very rewarding in your later life.

From Twenty-One to Thirty Years

Your twenties are the early morning of your life.
During this time there should not be any dark clouds or
    bad emotions to cover the sun of your clear and open mind.
A clear mind expresses a spiritually healthy soul.

This is not the time to sit and expect the gathering of harvest.
If you do, you are counting your chickens before they hatch!
It is a time to quietly concentrate on weeding, plowing, planting and growing.
The crops will be gathered at the right time after your appropriate and diligent care.

During this period, your life may be as impulsive as
    a galloping horse, dog or dragon.
Managing your energies is important so that
    you do not waste them to low impulses.

Therefore, avoid using your hands in meaningless fighting, rather
   use them to salute others in gestures of friendliness and respect.
Avoid using your mouth to express words of anger or displeasure.
Use your mouth to speak constructively of people, things and yourself.
Reciting short prayers may help you in this endeavor, such as:

> *I receive this birth for peace.*
> *Gentleness and harmony is my chosen being.*
> *I am not a tool for angry thought and motivation;*
>   *I am a student of the wisdom of the deep, blue sky.*
> *The blue sky above, with its bodies of light,*
>   *is my most important teacher in life.*

From Thirty-One to Forty Years

Now you have gathered the most physical strength of your life.
If you haven't then you should.
The sun has moved close to high noon,
   and the physical maturity of your life has arrived.
However, your mental maturity may be just beginning.

It is the time to do what should be done,
   and to be what you should be.
Whatever you do and be, you should be constructive.
If things are working constructively,
   then continue to progress forwards.

From Forty-One to Fifty Years

Although you are physically mature,
   your mind may only be like the half moon.
It is wrong to act as if the light is full and you know it all;
   far better to be a humble pupil of light.
A half moon is not brighter than a full moon.
Have you grown the objective vision of your mind?
That subtle light of wisdom is never affected by the shape of the moon.

You should effectively do what should be done before the
   period of late afternoon, and patiently wait for the fruit to ripen.
While you can rely on the movement of Nature to help your growth,
   it is mostly a result of your own efforts.
Keep steadily moving forwards until you have
   attained the full brightness of your mind.

From   Fifty-One   to   Sixty   Years

Now, as you continue to climb the ladder of life,
   you are almost exactly in the middle.
Do not lose patience and become frustrated with your progress,
   as grace comes from real maturity.
Although on its way, it has not yet fully arrived.
Neither should you become proud about your past experiences,
   as you have not yet reached the depth.
Simply stay open to know what is in front of you.

This period may feel a little awkward,
   since you are not very old, nor are you really young.
It is the right time for you to do your best in everything for which you strive.
But the best of your expectations may still be far away,
   so stay relaxed and steady.
You are making progress, and you can be where you wish to be.

From   Sixty-One   to   Seventy   Years

You are now entering a new stage of life.
Your wisdom should match the maturity of your physical changes.
But never think you are old, even though you may be able to live more inwardly.
To the inner world, you are still an infant.

Try to be pleasant with yourself when you do well, and
   improve those things with which you are uncomfortable.
Examine the consistency of yourself.
You may find there is some simplification to do.

Renew your life spiritually.
Life has to be conducted wisely now.

Accept that you may not be as wise as you thought you would be,
   and be proud that you have not grown into a fool either.
The difference between a wise man and a fool is
   that the fool likes to compete,
   while the wise work only to strengthen themselves.
The life of a wise person is not greatly affected by the outside world.

From Seventy-One to Eighty Years

Now is not the time to feel tired,
   as the maturity of your mind has just arrived.
It is not the time to blame others for the condition of your life.
However, it is the time to make self-corrections if you need to.
The good time of life is on its way.

Use no tension to solve tension, and
   use simplicity to handle complication.
Recognize that self-boasting can degrade the
   dignity of one's life, and self-pride gains no support.
Self-righteousness only invites resentment,
   while openness has the power to solve problems.
And know that laughter can dissolve obstacles.

From Eighty-One to Ninety Years

At this time, people may consider you mature.
But a real mature person tends to be childlike and
   cheerful no matter what situation they face,
   whereas a seemingly mature person tends to be
   childish and offers advice without request.
In the latter case, your seniority is discounted as meddlesome.

Rather than try to control the interests of the young,
  offer them more understanding, and transform
  your worries into the strength of healthy emotion.

At this time, before the beautiful sunset of your life,
  do not rush to compete with the light.
Relax instead and enjoy a cup of tea.

From   Ninety-One   to   One   Hundred   Years

You may be overly trained in social graces,
  but these do little for your natural life.
You may have forgotten how to open your mouth to yawn.
Have you been trained as a fool?

At this age, you tend to cough more and laugh less.
Have you made a mistake?
Both laughing and coughing help to reduce the gaseous pressure inside,
  but laughing is pleasant while coughing is annoying.
Learn to be pleasant rather than annoying.

From   One   Hundred   and   One   to
One   Hundred   and   Ten   Years

Live joyfully with the Sun.
Do not allow conventional religious teachers to paralyze the
  vigor of your life, and keep away from their professional suggestions
  that bid you to go to Heaven in order that they can make a living.
Understand that a good, strong soul is Heaven on Earth.
A deceived mind, however, never opens to this.

Regain an interest in visiting the mountains.
With their everlasting strength of natural life,
  they will inspire you not to fear the final stages of your physical life.

Help can also come from being with the little ones,
    as they always have something for you to learn.
By admiring their spirit of youthful independence,
    you can endeavor to take care of your daily life
    without relying on other people, and all sorts of medication.
That is really respecting life.

From One Hundred and Eleven to
One Hundred and Twenty Years

While it is important not to be young and stupid,
    it is just as important not to be an old fool.

The stupidity of youth comes from impulsivity,
    which may be the only asset of the young.
Unfortunately, only a few individuals know to constructively
    control it and guide it towards wisdom.
Value the impulse of life, and make proper use of it
    by transforming it into something useful for yourself and others.

The foolishness of an older person comes from stubbornness,
    but only crisis awaits the mind that loses flexibility.
No matter how old you are, stay open to the different views of others,
    except those who wish to comfort you by suggesting you are going to Heaven.
Far better that you strengthen your soul and detach from forms,
    both physical or conscious, as they are all illusory, and subject to change.
The changes remain far away from the everlasting, core reality of the soul.

Life is an interesting process.
When you are young, you need your parents to take care of you,
    but you should still nurture the spirit of independence
    in order to reduce your burden on them.
Then, when you are really old, you need your children to take care of you,
    but you should still endeavor to be spiritually independent,
    and rely on yourself as much as you realistically can.
This will help you grow stronger.

In the middle range of your life,
    it is natural to learn to take care of others.
This is a time when your parents or children require your help.
Though the young, and especially the older ones,
    are famous for their stubbornness,
    you should not deny your love because of it.
Excusing their stubbornness will make life more interesting.
Remember that even though you have made self-reliance your
    spiritual pursuit, and you have detached from external authority,
    interdependence in practical life is still a reality.

Within the shell of an egg, a young chick is prepared for life.
Similarly, within the shell of your physical life
    you are prepared for spiritual life.
Your body exists to support your spiritual pursuit.
When the time is ripe, you can break through the
    material shell, and launch off into the sky without attachments.
Presently, you are living in the shell of the
    material sphere, and by cooperating with Nature
    you can discover the source of your everlasting spiritual life.

It is important not to limit or harm your
    spiritual potential with gray thoughts and moods.
Appreciate that the Sun rises every day, and so can you.

You can visit your most faithful of friends,
    the sturdy mountains, to be encouraged.
They inspire you not to fear or worry, and
    to detach from the constant changes in the human ocean of life.

And remember to never be sentimental about your age,
    as the stones under your feet are much older than
    you, and have lived through more difficult times
    constantly being stamped on under people's feet.

PART IV

Serving the Mother Universe

We carry the conscious energy of the Mother Universe.
What can we do in return for her grace?

Chapter 23

Practice Universal Morality

The benign nature of human life has declined. People of the undeveloped world die for short-lived profits and unrighteous gain like flies in the dirt. They struggle with one another for positions of power and authority like wild dogs fighting over the remains of a dead animal. They rush around madly in the dark driven by low interests, like rats scurrying around in dark trenches. They live their life for such little worth. Some people, however, desire that from which most people run. They do not envy what other people envy, nor are they greedy for the power and authority for which most other people are greedy. These people have no interest in physical or social force, unlike those who rely on force. They prefer to practice universal morality in their lives. As a humble messenger of universal morality, I continually encourage people with better communication skills than myself to reach out and share in the enormous spiritual duty of improving the spiritual condition of humanity.

The single goal of the spiritual movement of the Integral Way, through its vehicle of the Path of Constructive Life (PCL), is to restore the understanding and sense of a universal moral life among all people. What this means simply is to be healthy and spiritually constructive. We encourage all people to appreciate and live with the constructive nature of the universe. Every generation needs simple, decent people, and the duty of any spiritual teaching is to support the decency and safety of all people of the world. Although there are different spiritual phases in a human life, the main pursuit up to around sixty years of age should be the restoration of the moral nature of life.

In the Integral Way of universal life, Tao is understood as the supportive nature of the universe, and Teh relates to its correct fulfillment in individual life. Teh is the accumulation of individual virtue. In other words, Tao is the Constructive Path of life, and Teh is the realization and application of that Constructive Path in one's everyday activity. Tao can also be understood as the unceasing pattern and flow of the forces of *yin* and *yang* in the endless expansion of the cosmos.

Tao, in the deep sense, is Universal Integral Truth. Once it is organized into a spiritual and cultural service, it becomes a life education for all generations. The

Integral Way is not composed of ready-made dogmas and static principles, although it does recommend discretion, prudence, and clear observation in all circumstances. This requires the growth and learning of life's wisdom.

Cultivating Tao as an individual duty of life is about minding the well-being of now, not yesterday, not tomorrow, but now. People who cultivate Tao do not cry over the spilt milk of yesterday, nor do they get excited for some great time that lies ahead. They focus on the well-being of now. Even if you live for a million years that longevity is still an accumulation of seconds.

The human spiritual effort is about merging Tao and Teh so they become one, as described by Lao Tzu in the *Tao Teh Ching*. Wise are those who find encouragement from the simplest *Tao Teh Ching* which expounds the Universal Way of life. Simplicity presents the essence, while great volumes merely elucidate.

In the *Tao Teh Ching*, Lao Tzu restructured the Yellow Emperor's vision of the universal Way of spiritual life. However, the practice of the Way as envisioned by Lao Tzu has not been fulfilled in China or anywhere else, except in some rural spiritual communities. And even though Jesus demonstrated the essence of the Way to the world by repaying evil with virtue, few people understood, let alone taught, his truth. Many people teach a level of immaturity that was taught to them by their undeveloped teachers. This is why the PCL has been formed to help people realize the plain and simple Way in their everyday life, and live Heaven on Earth.

Those with the devotion to help the voluntary work of this spiritual movement have been ordained as spiritual coaches and mentors. They have prepared themselves by thoroughly studying and working with the publications and teachings of the Way. They are willing to face the hardships of the world for this universal cause, and are unconcerned with how long their efforts will take. It may take many lifetimes.

The coaches and mentors of the PCL are individuals who live to deepen their understanding of natural life and universal health, and who offer their own healthy life in order to promote the health of the world. They embrace the universal kind spirit and virtues of Mother Nature, and practice these in their own lives and towards the lives of others. They are encouraged to succeed completely in all aspects of a healthy life, rather than only partially. They are not like un-developed people, who busily run after name and profit under the guise of a spiritual service. Their offering of service comes from their own spiritual appreciation that they share in the universal duty of helping humanity develop. Their service is not offered out of personal ambition or out of the need to earn a living; it is offered purely and voluntarily without asking for anything in return.

Coaches and mentors are guiding lights for the world. They, and other individu-als who live a universally constructive life, practice Tao in their respective societies by working to realize universal moral strength. Or, in other words, by working to help themselves and others live a universally constructive life. Universal moral-ity is the healthy strength of human society.

In support of their teaching services, they may adopt an improved style of west-ern religious service and structure. Although in realizing universal morality, high-est respect is given to those who remain anonymous for the meritorious deeds they do. Remaining anonymous is closer to the truth of Nature. However, at the general level of fulfillment it is better to give a name to the specific teaching organization or center for the purposes of transparency and accountability for what is being taught.

Coaches cultivate and rely on self-discipline, flexibility, and endurance in their personal and social lives. In order to realize Tao or the Way of universal morality in their personal lives, coaches do the following.

> Consider the health of the world to be just as important as the health of their lives.
>
> Treat the troubles of the world as their responsibility and work to solve them.
>
> Love serving the world not for any material or emotional reward, but in order to fulfill the healthy nature of life in their own lives.
>
> Spiritually develop themselves to be individuals of universal spiritual worth.

Bear the humiliation that no one else is able to bear for
the moral cause of universal love.

Face the trouble that no one else is able to face for the moral
cause of universal equality.

Accomplish that which no one else is able to accomplish for
the moral cause of universal righteousness.

Overcome the difficulty that no one else is able to overcome
for the moral cause of universal righteousness.

Triumph over what other people are unable to triumph over
for universal moral glory.

To help you fulfill a spiritual life and realize universal spiritual harmony, there
exist four important points which, together, with an individual, familial, and
socially-focused life form the best style of practice.

Appreciate spiritual life; it is essential. It should always be
a part of human life.

Appreciate spiritual education; it is necessary. A true spiritual
education helps people manage and refine their wild nature.

Appreciate spiritual leadership; it is a gift. A true spiritual leader
guides people in the direction of universal spiritual harmony.

Appreciate spiritual congregations; these are important. A true
congregation is where people can come together to worship and
offer piety towards the high God of Universal Spiritual Unity.
Attending this kind of weekly service helps you maintain your
spiritual health.

Chapter 24

Offer Healthy Spiritual Service

A spiritual teaching requires two things to effectively serve humanity. One is a healthy spiritual education based on high universal principles that apply to all people, and the other is a correctly guided warmth or enthusiasm to realize those principles for the goodwill of all. However, before society can move towards a common universal spiritual direction, we must clear away the cultural and religious confusion and gather together the positive contributions. Becoming aware of the difference between universal and partial principles will help us in this endeavor. Universal principles apply to all people in all circumstances and have lasting value, whereas partial approaches have only temporary value applying to some people and some societies in certain circumstances.

Not everyone has grown to understand the value of accepting and pursuing universal principles, even though these are obviously needed for humanity's health and safety. Some people cannot yet see that it is the universal nature that provides all lives with an equal opportunity to survive. This is why the Integral Way, through the Path of Constructive Life (PCL), offers a universal spiritual teaching that helps people become aware of the plain truth in their everyday lives.

The objective of the Integral Way is to guide people back to the universal nature and pure soul. It helps people to appreciate that everyone is a part of one family, and to realize that the Universal Nature, or God, helps those who help themselves. When people recognize that humanity is one family and shares in the same big life, they will naturally direct their enthusiasm to fulfill universal spiritual principles in their lives as the only worthwhile direction to pursue.

The Integral Way promotes respect for and harmony with the deep substance of the Mother Universe and her subtle laws and virtues. Although she is difficult to follow exactly, at the very least we can spiritually align ourselves with her moral attributes such as health, balance, broadness, harmony, openness, constructivism, centeredness, cooperation, mutual support, and mutual accomplishment. It is unnatural when the offspring do not resemble their mother. Therefore, our human health should cohere to the health of the Mother Universe. Finding balance in our lives is at the heart of our goal to be healthy.

The purpose of the PCL is to gather together its many decades of modern spiritual service and offer it in a convenient package for people. This is so everyone can use it in order to understand how to align with universal morality and live a complete life of health in body, mind, spirit, morals, and finance. The decision to follow the PCL is based on self-selection, rather than any type of persuasion or imposition. In the past, religious choices were based on one's emotional or sentimental inclination, whereas the teachings of the Integral Way are based on the healthy, safe, and complete development of the individual.

At the basic level of attainment, followers of the PCL achieve physical, mental, and spiritual well-being. At the medium level, they achieve those three aspects as well as moral and financial health. The basic expression of financial health is self-reliance. The greatest achievement is to attain all five healths, as well as to selflessly contribute to the spiritual and moral health of humanity. This can be accomplished by offering organized spiritual services and teachings that are appropriate to the surroundings and which are carried out alongside one's self-supported and constructive life. Spiritually, the goal is to achieve the self-mastery of life, internally and externally.

A potential master is someone who has grown beyond their small ego self. They carry the sense of being a spiritual mast or guide for the ship of the world. They live a spiritually constructive and universally moral life. Spiritually, they remain naive and innocent like a newborn babe, whose spiritual potency is almost the same as that of the subtle origin of the universe. The mind of a master is pure and contains only universal constructive energy. Their hearts are open to the care of the Mother Universe, which they receive by living earnestly and honestly in her cradle.

The new centers or congregations that grow up in the faith of the Mother Universe are spiritual coopportunities of the Integral Way. The centers can form branches or members of the Integral Way Society (IWS). They serve to help you and others realize the five healths in life. Various tools are offered to help people break through their mental and emotional obstacles, in order to open their minds and nurture their spirit. With less emotion, an open mind, and healthy foundation, people have more of an opportunity to become aware of universal principles and safely pursue the deep wisdom of life.

The Center is led by a spiritual host or hostess, who is a mentor or coach of the Integral Way. The mentors and coaches have chosen to share their spiritual life with others as part of their universal spiritual duty. They have enlarged the spiritual sense of themselves to include all people of the world. Those who are naturally attracted to the center, come together under the guidance of the mentors and coaches to share and mutually assist one another to live a life of complete health.

The center resembles a spiritual family, or self-responsible spiritual community, which actualizes the truth that the universal nature helps those who help themselves. Its members are role models for those serious and sincere people who wish to lead a spiritually clean, healthy, and self-responsible life, and who wish to identify with the spirit of the Mother Universe.

For the public service, the mentors and coaches draw from the universal teachings of the Integral Way. They introduce healthy thoughts, visions, and practical activities, to stimulate and inspire the universal spiritual growth of those who join the gatherings. The spiritual educational services of the center promote the understanding that the profound universal nature is the human spiritual nature. Members are encouraged to spiritually cultivate in order to develop their universal nature. Respect and piety is thus offered towards the Mother Universe as the source and support of all life. By worshipping her with a sincere and pure heart, humanity can gradually regain its healthy heart. God is newly recognized as the universal conscience, and natural child-like joy is appreciated as the healthiest emotional expression of life and foremost discipline. Natural joy is the nature of the Mother Universe. It is the loudest nonverbal prayer we can offer her.

The everyday activities of the teachers and members of the various centers, whether emotional, physical, financial, or spiritual, are guided by whether they are constructive for the well-being of oneself and others. Various ceremonies and spiritual practices can be adopted from the teachings of the Integral Way in support of individual and group health, as long as such activities are not overdone or overly formalized. The ceremonies and practices remind you to respect your inner health through maintaining a clean body, eating clean food, and enjoying harmonious and cooperative relationships with other people and with Mother Nature. The activities can vary according to the rhythmic activity of life, the seasonal changes, and the different goals for the different stages of an individual's life.

The spiritual community of the PCL considers all people to be children of the Mother Universe. Its members are therefore encouraged to take an interest in the healthy and positive spiritual customs of other traditions, including their style of clothing and cuisine. By taking an interest in new things and trying them out, one can appreciate and understand how humans move through variety both before and after they reach the depth of universal spirituality. Beneficial spiritual customs can be adopted or rotated in the various centers, provided they are appropriate to the spiritual mission of improving humanity's spiritual health.

The following books are recommended as the spiritual foundation of the various centers: *The Majestic Domain of the Heart*; *The Centermost Way* as the essential spiritual guide for the public; *Enrich Your Life with Virtue* as the new theology of inner spiritual and virtuous development, which replaces the conventional and imaginary concepts of an external divinity; *The Foundation of a Happy Life*, and the six books in the *Constructive Life* series, of which this book is one.[1]

Followers of the Integral Way cultivate themselves to understand and value more and more deeply that while living and appreciating their worldly life they are, at the same time, on an unchartered voyage of the Milky Way. Most people fail to recognize the infinite nature of their life. This is because they become overly occupied with their life's problems and blindly follow the limited vision of their social leaders. The Integral Way works to expand people's vision, so they can recognize the value of cooperating together and following universal high principles. This is so they can travel smoothly towards the light of the Mother Universe. Those who give their hands to help in this progress are people of universal conscience; they are people of God.

---

1. All the books mentioned in this paragraph are available from SevenStar Communications, Los Angeles, at http://www.sevenstarcom.com, or http://www.taoofwellness.com.

Chapter 25

The Twelve Commitments of the Mother Universe

Loyally fulfill the Universal Integral Way in your life. One who lives a developed life has a universal concern which transcends personal interest.

Move dutifully out of the darkness into the light of life. In the darkness, all you feel is your own existence. In the light, you appreciate and respect other people, and conduct your life appropriately and value it completely. This includes having a healthy body; a warm, kind heart; a clear, open mind; a universal moral personality; ethics in finance, and a consistency of watching over these to ensure they remain balanced.

Cultivate positive strength. Persistently cultivate the positive strength of life and merge your personal fortune with the eternal Way of life. No matter how fortunate you are, you may still encounter obstacles in life, both visible and invisible. If you have already suffered from such things then make a concerted effort not to continue your old habits, or interests, so as not to encounter bigger obstacles. Learn to move away from the bumpy road of life and accept a new destiny of living with the Way. You may have already paid a high price to obtain a life of far less worth.

Practice kindness so as not to create trouble for yourself or others. Although you have an individual destiny, you also are a part of a local or common social destiny. In the hands of a virtueless leader, many innocent lives can be made to suffer or die, as in Germany and Japan during the Second World War, and in China during the so-called cultural revolution. Those tragic situations were the result of egotistical power struggles.

Practice universal love towards all people. Your personal fortune is related to the fortune of others. As a member of a society, you either enjoy or suffer the actions of your society, which could be progressive, recessive or depressive. Therefore, contribute to society in a way that is supportive rather than burdensome or draining. Even though we encourage you to positively fulfill your duty as a social citizen, we recommend you broaden your vision to appreciate and embrace humanity as one big family. Developed individuals teach you to love the human race broadly. This is the real practice of universal love. If you wish to read more about the spiritual direction of humanity read *The Uncharted Voyage Towards the Subtle Light.*

Remain a faithful and permanent pupil of Everlasting Life and Truth. Save yourself and the world by accepting the Integral Way with its subtle universal law as the only true authority in life. To understand more about the subtle law, read *The Subtle Universal Law and the Integral Way of Life.*[1]

Behave righteously and rationally in life. Conflict, no matter what kind—financial, political, ideological, or religious—is mostly due to immaturity or lack of development. The more you grow, the less argumentative you become. You should avoid inciting or supporting trouble of any kind, and never apply your intellectual capability negatively or wickedly. Most of the world's troubles are created by people who misuse their intelligence. The majority of societies are composed of undeveloped people who do not endeavor to grow and understand that they are responsible for their own creations. Due to all this irresponsible mischief the world is degraded.

Be a Light Guard in your own life and for the world. I assign to you all the role of Light Guard. Another term for Light Guard is human conscience. Though subtle, you need to develop your conscience to be pure and clear. Next to the breath of life it is the most precious thing that the Mother Universe has given you. Do your best to keep away from creating difficulties and engaging in any negative sporting or mischievous activities.

Live in the Light of the Integral Way. Peacefully fulfill the new destiny of humanity in order to live in the light with harmony, cooperation, and mutual support. To live in the light means to eliminate war of any kind. It is a way of being where all people and races positively contribute their strength to make the world a better place for all to live as a unified whole. Therefore, instead of trying to escape to some religious Heaven, people can live and enjoy Heaven on Earth. Thus, do not rush to take sides in either small conflicts or big wars. It is more appropriate to

---

1. This and the previously mentioned book are available from SevenStar Communications, Los Angeles, at http://www.sevenstarcom.com, or http://www.taoofwellness.com.

allow trouble to stay limited to its size, and the dust of war to settle down by itself. It is best to be an independent observer and maintain the moral strength of the universe. This means not to allow your life to be drawn into meaningless conflict, even among your family and friends. Fighting, arguing, and meddling are the daily content of undeveloped lives. When you refrain from supporting trouble of any kind, true peace and happiness is sure to prevail.

Be balanced. Practice balance in your life and avoid excessiveness or extremes of any kind.

Practice nondiscrimination. Adopt an equal and nondiscriminating attitude towards the various social customs of the world, whether they are your own or another's. Do not use social customs in competitive ways, but allow people to grow at their own pace. Withdraw from situations where extremes are practiced and conflict exists. People who are overly involved in such things have lost the common, good sense of life. It is appropriate to walk away from the entrapment of conventional mistakes.

Offer selfless service. Offer your selfless service by learning from the Mother of Heaven, the Earth, all natural deities, and decent, balanced people with their useful and constructive creations. This is the highest commitment of the sages. Universal beings such as Moses, Jesus, Mohammed, and Buddha exemplified what it means to have universal concern for the people of their area and time. Now it is your turn to do the same or better.

In order to move away from your old life patterns and realize the twelve commitments, there are three stages through which to progress.

In the first stage, you may have been on the bumpy road of life, but with self-awareness you know how not to create new bumps. With a clear and deepening perception you are able to notice the bumps, and with psychological growth you can slow them down and reduce their associated shock. Gradually, you learn how not to attract them. By learning the Universal Way of life, you strengthen your vitality so that you can remove troublesome habits, dissolve feelings that relate to being troubled by others, and cope better with the world.

In the second stage, you have modified your personal interests and personal pursuits, so money, power, physical pleasure, and material comforts are no longer central to your existence. Though you may still obtain these and enjoy them, you are no longer enslaved or attached to them. Instead, you enjoy spiritual freedom above all. This is how you are able to uplift yourself out of the old pattern of being annoyed or troubled by life.

In the third stage, you have said goodbye to the old destiny of life. You now begin to live a new destiny whereby you merge the small interests of your life to the greater life of the universe. You are beginning to live with the universal nature and its eternal supportive energy.

Chapter 26

Be a Universal Citizen

Citizens of the Mother Universe:

> Do not need to be formally initiated, but they do need to sincerely
> and consistently pursue universal spiritual unity.

> Are consciously free, independent, and possess a broad and whole
> personality. In other words, they have freed themselves from all
> enslavements.

> Are transreligious and, at the same time, are above all worldly
> religions, though they may still use some type of religious structure
> to help serve the world.

> Transcend all forms of social bonds such as race, nationality, religion,
> politics, and family.

> Are completely capable of facing the Mother Universe without any
> form of identity such as name or title.

> Are morally obligated and responsible for the health of the world.
> If they teach people, they do so using a form or no form according
> to what they are sincerely able to do.

> Live in the world without any attachments and by earning a decent
> income from a dignified source.

> Accept the society, government, and local customs of their area for
> what they are without making trouble, while at the same time diligently
> maintaining their inner pursuit of universal spiritual citizenship.

> Dignify their lives by accepting only those things which come to
> them naturally and peacefully without competition and struggle.

> Face the Mother Universe with the purity of a newborn babe,
> and without owing anything to the world or themselves. They do
> not subject their soul to limiting concepts of God, Allah, or Buddha,
> and so forth.

Never boast of their attainments nor need to prove themselves
to anyone. They fulfill their life quietly with balance and harmony.

Have no need to prove that they are of a higher spiritual stature
than other people.

Accept difficulties and challenges as the nutrition to help purify
and strengthen their soul so that they are able to soar high spiritually.

Are completely aware of the difference between the conditioned
acquired mind and the pure spirit. They understand that an overly
active mind hardens the spirit. Thus they do not engage in mental
fantasy and illusory thinking. When the mind ceases to be active,
the spirit becomes effective.

Understand that while true spiritual work and true spiritual
pursuit is formless, most people require some form of spiritual teaching.
That is why a universal citizen uses the teachings of the Integral Way
through its vehicle of the Path of Constructive Life (PCL).

Have deep and socially independent views of universal morality.
However, while they may not agree with everything their society
does, they have no need to emphasize differences or insist on their way
because they observe the operation of the subtle universal law in their
lives. As a universal citizen and exemplar of the teachings of the
Integral Way, one lives and works constructively with the
universal nature.

Accomplish all of the above without telling anyone.

Although a universal citizen becomes achieved in all seventeen fulfillments above,
they still need to live in the world. They therefore accommodate themselves to
its current state of development without complaint or resentment. Socially serving the Integral Way is about living in harmony with all kinds of people. This is
an essential part of the daily work of the Way.

At the external level, most societies establish ethical standards and social disci-
plines for their people. Each society is different. In China, over 4,000 years ago,
Emperor Shun established five ethical goals which shaped the cultural direction
and social behavior of the Chinese at the general external level. Those are:

Towards one's parents express filial piety.

Towards one spouse offer love and care.

Towards one's siblings offer respect and support.

Towards one's friends offer appropriate assistance.

Towards the local social order offer cooperation and obedience.

I recommend you use Shun's model to guide your external life, and use the seventeen fulfillments above to guide your inner spiritual pursuit.

There are other universal citizens who fulfilled their moral duty to their society in different ways, responding to the needs of their people. Lao Tzu fulfilled his universal duty differently to Shun, suggesting that people live in harmony with Mother Nature.

I appreciate and respect what other universal beings such as Zoroaster, Jain, Shakyamuni, Jesus, Mani, and Mohammed did for their people and the world, and consider their work as stages in the development of the world. However, their teachings (some of which were never written down) became heavily formalized, and were used by people for limited purposes. Be aware that any form and establishment that is overly tight, restricts and binds the human spirit. People become too easily attached to the form and neglect the real essence of the teachings. People who think that the formal teaching is the essence have misunderstood the real teaching of those universal individuals. They fail to see that true spiritual work is far beyond the form.

The nature of a natural, healthy life, and the real value of social establishments is described in the following poem, which dates from the time of Emperor Yao (2333–2224 BCE), when people were naturally gentle and kind.

When the sun rises it's time for me to work.
When the sun sets it's time for me to rest.
I chisel a well for my drinking, and beat the ground for my merry-making.
What does my life have to do with kings and religious salvation?

In today's world, the natural environment is disrespected and polluted, and conflict is considered part of the normal fabric of life. What people really need is more opportunity for making friends, earning a healthy income, achieving a good living, and making genuine spiritual progress. They should be able to freely exchange their spiritual experiences and life knowledge internationally, nationally, and locally. That is why we recommend a natural and universal way of life, unfettered by restrictive social or government policies.

Universal moral qualities are particularly supportive when living in a troubled world. By attuning yourselves to universal morality, health, peace, cooperation, mutual help, and natural orderliness grows within and among all lives.

The pursuit of a universal spiritual life does not pull people away from their social duties or divorce them from their government. But it does encourage the understanding that in relation to self-adjustment, being natural and humanistic is the first moral principle to follow, whereas being patriotic and faithful to social customs whether religious, familial or otherwise, is the second moral principle to follow. The first moral principle, which is universal, is being impartial, non-dualistic, and equally kind to all. This is what we encourage you to practice within your communities and with all people.

Worldly authorities encourage people to favor their social customs at the expense of a natural and humanistic way of life. The universal moral principle suggests you respect the local customs, and follow them using your independent and objective discernment, while still holding firmly to the first moral principle. Your inner discernment will grow through the rational and spiritual development of your life.

A healthy spirituality is a balanced view of life. It is universally, socially, and personally health-focused. It serves all people who practice self-evaluation and self-cultivation. You can begin by listing the virtues and fulfillments above, and evaluate yourself honestly. You may discover that your local spirituality fits the second moral principle. The Integral Way recommends you uphold universal moral virtue as the first principle, and not sacrifice it to any false way of living as most people do. If you live in a false living situation, shut your mouth and continue to develop your inner life privately paying serious attention to the sixteenth fulfillment above.

Lastly and importantly, the few names that I have quoted in this chapter are noble souls who achieved universal citizenship, despite the formal burden and false conditioning of their times. After they quit the shell of their life, the Mother Universe embraced their souls for the work of brightening the souls of others.

Chapter 27

Realize Universal Love

The Mother of the Universe is the heart of the universe. Love is the healthy energy of the heart.

In human expression, love is a word that is frequently used, but that does not mean it is always correctly applied. It is important that one clearly understands that universal love is the spiritual expansion and the spiritual merit of life, whereas personal love relates to the much narrower scope of personal life.

Universal, public love refers to one's spiritual merit and virtuous achievement, whereas personal love tends to be emotional and based on unnatural creations. Success in personal love comes through the management of one's desires and emotions. In personal love, your love should be based on your partner's undecorated personality. But whether public or personal, love should be peaceful. The two qualities of love and peace go together. When one is absent, the other is absent too.

In all normal circumstances of worldly life, the most reliable love is motherly love. Motherly love is unconditional. This unconditional quality is the power that supports the life of the universe. Motherly love is the highest quality of love in human life and natural lives. Therefore, it should be recognized that love comes from Nature. Natural love is the truest love and the most reliable support for all existence. Natural love is harmonizing without being demanding. A healthy human society is an extension of Nature's love.

> With universal love, there is hope for peace and progress.
>
> With universal love, all life is respected and loved.
>
> With universal love, all difficulties can be overcome.
>
> With universal love, all troubles can be removed and all misunderstandings dissolved.

With universal love, no personal emotion or desire is insisted upon or pushed to an extreme.

With universal love, righteousness is always the first to be considered in all human behaviors.

With universal love, no nation, race, or individual, bullies another nor expands themselves at the expense of another's safety.

With universal love, the minds of people are brightened so that no darkness remains.

With universal love, good, moral people are put in responsible positions, whereas virtueless people are asked to step aside.

With universal love, no job is considered unworthy when it is done correctly.

With universal love, no one starves.

With universal love, no life is lost.

With universal love, all people are protected.

With universal love, the fountain of wisdom never ceases to flow smoothly.

With universal love, no dark force lasts long.

With universal love, the stubborn become willing to open.

With universal love, the foolish can be enlightened.

With universal love, all people are treated equally.

With universal love, no hatred is considered unforgivable.

With universal love, no one is considered unworthy of help.

With universal love, no temporal darkness can discourage the steady and enduring progress of universal morality.

With universal love, the health of society is attended to responsibly.

With universal love, all people unite as one and work cooperatively together for a harmonious world.

With universal love, night can be day. A diligent, spiritual worker is therefore able to work in the semi-darkness of a ship's cabin, as it sails across the ocean to reach the shore on the other side at dawn.

With the universal heart and the fullness of love, the world is open and ready for all good things to evolve.

Chapter 28

Prayers for Spiritual Study Groups

O p e n i n g   P r a y e r

Universal Divine Oneness,
    we are gathered here in your heart with our hearts
    to cleanse, purify, and revitalize ourselves.

Living in today's world,
    we have been conditioned to be busy-minded,
    rushed, and pushy-minded.
The negative elements of life have blinded us from seeing you.
You, however, are everywhere.
You are in all life and all life is in you.

The orderliness of the universe is not a human creation.
The healthy order of our lives comes from you and lies with you.
How can we live without your life-giving vitality?

It is the foremost ignorance of humans
    to dare to imply that a capable man's image
    can be the creator of the world.
Those people created a list of jobs for the
    imagined creator to do from day one to day seven.
How could God have the need to live in the
    same time-frame as the earthling thinkers?

Everyone is born natural.
Wise are those who know the limits of their physical life,
    and who know the boundless reaching out of the spiritual life
    to embrace their true being as the One Unlimited Life.

Universal Divine Oneness,
*   we beseech your support for our wish*
*   to eliminate all the negativity from human spirituality.*
That is our only intention of personalizing you.
Other people have exalted you for selfish purposes.
Their intention of privatizing you was done for
*   the purposes of competing between one another,*
*   and between one religion and another.*
But even those people know that you are everywhere,
*   because your presence cannot be limited to*
*   Jerusalem, Mecca, the Vatican, or indeed to any place.*

Your presence is just here simply with us.
Then what do people fight for?
They fight for the private enterprise.
For hundreds of years people have played those
*   immature games and now it's enough.*

We sympathize with the efforts of those people who,
*   in the early stages and at different times of humanity,*
*   sought to bring some order to an unruly world.*
Now is the time for all people to recognize the simple universal fact
*   that the fault of the world's negative spiritual condition*
*   does not lie with the true origins of worldly religions,*
*   it lies with the socialization of religions.*
Especially if those social religions continue to insist on the
*   negative tendency of privatizing and monopolizing*
*   the One Universal Spiritual Reality.*

The universal religious spirits
*   of people—the God in people—should not be privatized.*
The universal spiritual quality is the true foundation of
*   all people's spiritual lives, including those who deny God.*
*   It is one spiritual expression.*
Even atheists may express closeness to God.
Why? Because anyone's eyes can see the eyes by the eyes.

We are determined to strengthen ourselves to
   defend and protect the Universal Spiritual Oneness.
We accept the challenge of constructive debate from anyone.

We are gathered here to listen to, discuss with,
   learn from, and absorb your universal being.
With utmost sincerity and love,
   we request your inspiration and enlightenment.

Closing Prayer

Universal Divine Oneness,
Thank you for conducting this meeting
   without designs, details, or plans.
You are the best design.
You are the ultimate plan.
You even conducted this meeting
   without the physical presence of a teacher,
   for the teacher knows that
   you are the greatest Teacher above all.

We all clearly know that you are
   inside of us and outside of us.
As your children, we just want to be close to you.
We want to be in your Heart.
You are vividly in our hearts.

With utmost sincerity,
   we express love to one another,
   and with all voices as one voice
   we express love to you,
   endless love.

PART V

Prayers to the Universal Mother

Dear Universal Mother,
Thank you for providing me with everything.

Chapter 29

The Value of Our Existence

Over the past 25 years, I have used over one hundred books and many speaking opportunities to respond to people who are in different situations and stages of life. The purpose of my work is to support the spiritual self-cultivation and self-improvement of everyone. My focus has been to prepare individuals to help themselves. At this stage, some of them are ready to offer themselves as voluntary teachers for extensive social service and the promotion of a universal faith.

The study of my books has been a form of spiritual reflection for them. Now it is time for them to help others do the same by spreading the message of confidence in the healthy nature of life. Their own lives are healthy since they have constantly worked on self-improvement. They also spread the message of confidence in the Universal Nature as the source and support of all life.

We need to grow continually and do better in order to help the general public reach mental and spiritual health through the genuine support of the spiritual teachings of the Integral Way. We need to reach the majority of people and help them realize the benefit of spiritual self-improvement and spiritual self-cultivation. We can do this by communicating simply and clearly, and by inspiring those around us to embrace the universal supportiveness of Nature. For this reason, we have started placing more emphasis on Tao as the Way of the Mother of the Universe. Although she is nonbeing, she is the mother of all beings and all energy beings. Tao is the Way and the Way is the Mother of All Universes.

We do not intend to imitate the old approach of conventional religious teachers who personified aspects of Nature in their establishment of religions. That kind of religion is built on a limited and partial vision of great Nature. It leads to separation among people, and limits them to the conceptual cages of their teacher's mental creation.

The Integral Way's inherited faith, which is over a million years old, is that the entire universe is one big life, while humans are the small life within it. With this fact in mind, it is proper to address the Way of Integral Truth as the Mother of Nature or the Mother of the Universe.

Since the Dragon Year of 2000, and during my recent trips to south Asia, Australia, and New Zealand, I offered the following three invocations of the Mother of the Universe to whomever I met. I was also inspired to produce a number of versions of My Humble Prayer to the Universal Mother. I have instructed the newly completed Taoist Global Mission to gather financial strength in order to entrance the new Dragon energy of our social service.

We need this new approach to help humanity develop spiritually. I offer these invocations and this book for all to use as the new spiritual model for the world. You can select one or several invocations and use them flexibly for your own self-improvement and internal support. When the opportunity arises, you can make copies to give to your friends in order to help uplift the spiritual condition of humanity.

Invocation for Soul Protection and Upliftment (Version I)

Goddesses of Mercy, please help me.
Goddesses of Mercy, please help me.
Goddesses of Mercy, please help me.

Your child beseeches your boundless love and light.

Please help me understand the value that my life brings to existence.
Help me develop self-awareness in order to respect my own being
*   among all other beings.*
Bestow your light and wisdom on me
*   so that I do not engage in self-abusive activities,*
*   nor involve myself in things that would poison my nature.*

Guide me to be my best and truest self.
Show me how to work within positive circumstances
*   and how to turn away from negative traps.*

Enable me to help those who have less.
May I accomplish this in ways that do not deplete those
   who have more nor create harm.
May I hold no bitterness or envy towards those who have more,
   and may I not be arrogant if I happen to be more fortunate than others.
Allow me to learn the value of being humble
   and of not provoking negativity in others.

Strengthen me if I momentarily fall behind
   and if I happen to make progress,
   enable me to bring peace and safety to those who suffer.

With utmost sincerity,
   may I reach the most responsive divine source,
   the Mother of All Universes.

Invocation for Soul Protection and Upliftment (Version II)

Goddesses of Mercy, please hear me.

Your boundless love and light inspire your devoted child.
Through your enlightenment, I understand the value of my life
   and my existence in relationship to others.

With your help, I develop the self-awareness that enables me
   to respect my own being in the midst of worldly life.
Please accept my deep appreciation for the light of your
   grace and wisdom that shines upon me,
   helping me to avoid engaging in self-abusive activities
   or involving myself in things that would poison my life.

I guide my life to express my best and truest self.
I learn how to work within positive circumstances
   and how to turn away from negative traps.

You enable me to help those who have less
  and to do so in ways that do not deplete those who have more.
I hold no bitterness or envy towards those
  who have more or who do better in life,
  thus I accomplish this without causing any harm.

I am empowered by the unselfish spiritual quality of a mother
  who cares for and serves her children without seeking reward.

If I happen to be more fortunate than others, I practice humility.
Through a correct attitude and approach,
  I avoid stirring up negativity in others.

Your example strengthens me,
  when I am tempted to fall behind.

Through realizing the truth of my own nature,
  I am able to bring peace and safety to those
  who suffer from self-created or worldly trouble.
I do not evade the duty of my own self-delivery,
  while I work towards the delivery of all.

With utmost sincerity,
  may I reach the most responsive divine source,
  the Mother of All Universes.

Invocation for Soul Protection
and Upliftment (Version III)

Goddesses of Mercy, please help me.
Goddesses of Mercy, please help me.
Goddesses of Mercy, please help me.

Your child beseeches your boundless love and light.
Please help me to understand the value of my life among all existences.

In the light of your wisdom,
I do not engage in self-abusive activities
nor do I involve myself in things that would poison my nature.
Guide me to be my best self.
Guide me to contemplate my life deeply and to see whether or not
I have brought difficulty to those who love me.

Allow my appreciation for you and for the spiritual nature of all mothers
to grow past my inexperience and insensitivity.
Thank you for allowing me to witness the tender care
and inexhaustible love of mothers towards their children,
which they offer without expecting any reward.
Also, allow me to have more understanding of those mothers in this generation
who have been confused by their personal life situations.
In my role as a son or daughter, help me to know not to expect my own mother
to be an expert and possess all knowledge and skill to raise me,
or to have had the experience of raising a dozen children
before giving birth to me.
If I do not learn to love and understand my mother,
how can I love and understand other individuals in this world?

As an adult, if I can have even the smallest spiritual growth,
I will help both mothers and children to live naturally.
I will be responsible for my own spiritual well-being and
I will not become overly dominating towards other lives.
Help me to avoid the domination that causes love and caring to become negative.
Help me to avoid this rough and unpolished practice in today's society,
seen widely in homes, schools, governments, religions, and other areas.
Help me to learn to understand the different situations of life
so that spiritual forgiveness will grow in my heart.
May the great power of forgiveness be the number one blessing in my life.

With utmost sincerity,
may I reach the most responsive divine source,
the Mother of All Universes.

Chapter 30

Feminine Virtue Naturally Guides Masculine Strength

(From northern New Zealand)

Dear Universal Mother,
As I sit by your oceanside,
  allow your tide to wash me clean,
  and allow my reflections on the journey of human life
  to be expressed clearly here.

In the long, early stages of humanity,
  people respected Nature as the big background of
  and major influence on their life.
Fearing Nature's uncontrollable forces,
  some people began to create prayers and symbolic practices
  in order to communicate with and affect her mystical force.
These actions attracted the attention of others
  who entrusted to those people the settling of
  minor disputes and the making of social decisions.

In the beginning, it was women
  who were naturally more perceptive than men,
  though men had more physical strength.
Over time, the women taught their subtle arts to their children,
  both girls and boys.
As boys grew to be men, they gradually took over the
  spiritual activity of women while continuing their physical warrior role.
From the aggressive and competitive nature of men,
  the desire for expansion increased.
Activities that used to be commanded by spiritual individuals
  began to be governed by warriors themselves.
Political structures and hierarchies were formed, and society shifted
  from being more peaceful, cooperative, and mother-centered
  to being more dominating, controlling, and father-centered.

This situation, which has lasted for around 4,000 years,
   has led to much trouble.

The male leaders, in order to enhance their rule and raise a new social order,
   sought support from spiritual faith.
Men trained in spiritual work began to play an important social role,
   and the worship of different deities was created
   to fit and support people's different psychological needs.
Social religion and a tight social control were formed
   that continue to this day.

In many societies, religious practices form a familiar part of life,
   and they have become symbols for social morality.
Even though positive social progress has been made,
   there is still a great deal of religious competition
   that fuels the movement towards excessive materialism, over-control,
   and social competition.
The value of a natural life is not recognized as a spiritual focus,
   nor is spiritual self-improvement appreciated
   as the important center of each individual.
Responsible leaders should understand that too much social establishment,
   whether materialistic or religious, creates social pressure that harms the natural,
   healthy life force of people and society.

In the early stages of human life,
   when females were spiritual and social leaders,
   life was more harmonious.
The feminine principles of cooperation and gentleness
   were valued and respected.
However, once the competitive and aggressive nature of men came to power,
   our human relationship with Nature grew weak
   and the balance and harmony of life declined.
Today, political and religious conflict and competition is a much stronger feature
   in our lives than our pure spiritual relationship with Nature.
In an overwhelming sea of social troubles,
   we no longer feel Nature's support and guidance.

I devote myself to bringing about an understanding among people
    that natural spiritual reality is the common background of all human societies,
    and that there is great benefit in spiritual self-improvement.
It brings happiness and joy to life.
To restore peace and harmony to an unbalanced and degraded world,
    my main suggestion has been to restore one's faith in Nature and recognize that:

The Sky is my Father.
The Earth is my Mother.
All people are my brothers and sisters.
With the support and protection of all gods and deities,
    I can enjoy living in the heart
    of the Great Mother of the Universe.

All my books are offerings to those who wish to learn
    how to improve themselves spiritually and live the Integral Way of natural life.

As children of the Mother Universe,
    we can appreciate the fact that one cannot know very much
    if one is overly self-interested.
Life can be enormous if one knows how to devote oneself
    to developing benevolence towards all life.

A life that contains spiritual value benefits all people.
Such a life does not care anymore for a noisy way of being.
Such a life has achieved itself through spiritual self-improvement
    that is not optional and is a great service to all life.
Real life experiences and deep life learning can be the true support
    of anyone's life, and an invaluable service to others.

My training was in the integral healing work of natural medicine
    that developed from the natural society of ancient China.
The aim of my work is to restore complete health
    to the lives of all people and the world.
Far from being a personal ambition, it is my personal sharing
    and humble response to the need of humanity.

Chapter 31

Be Gallant in Life

(From Muriwai, New Zealand)

Most respected Mother of the Universe,
You dwell within the tiny details of daily life,
    as well as in the boundless surrounding infinity.
Your being is hard to recognize for those
    who hold on tight to a partial view of life.

People think they know the truth of life with great certainty.
What they don't see is how their perceptions and conceptual abilities
    are limited by their experiences and technological creations.
The more they develop their partial views,
    the harder it becomes to see things broadly.
As people come to know the small and overlook the broad,
    they become more assertive of the small.
This is how rigid social beliefs are established,
    and how arguments and fights occur.
So much trouble occurs because people insist on
    their partial views over that of others.
The broader one's views become, however,
    the less assertive one needs to be.

I am just a baby who has made a breakthrough
    that allows me to see through the intellectual walls and go beyond.
I wish to share this attainment with other babies so they may also understand.
I need to explain in words that relate to their
    knowledge and experience in this small world.
I can communicate that which their experiences
    allow them to understand.

Dear Mother,
I wish to carry this message of yours to them:

Be happy with the nature of life and move with the Sky and Earth.
Do not overly trust conceptual creations or beliefs
*   as these only lead to darkness.*

Dear Mother,
Thank you for the gifts you offer.
You provide us with the opportunity of life.
You provide us with the opportunity of development.
You provide us with the opportunity of unlimited transformation.
Thank you for your kindness and love.

With your light, we come to understand that life is an opportunity,
*   not an obstacle or a hurdle to be placed in Nature's way.*
Rather, life can express a higher level of energy flow.
We humans can attract the good fruits of life
*   through our healthy and appropriate creations.*

With your light, we can realize the opportunity you bestow.
Inspired, we can realize our life as it should be and, in this way,
*   become creative, prosperous, and enjoy life's just rewards.*

Even if life is hard, we may still find balance in having the things we like.
As accomplishments are made, these may lead to further accomplishments.
A retreat may be used to gain fresh, creative energy and renewed accomplishments.
As our life experiences accumulate, our creativity also increases.

For the one who intends to master life,
*   there are various stages of transformation*
*   that can be experienced at different times.*
As a tiny dot of life is attached to a leaf, so is the caterpillar formed.
Later, a chrysalis appears and from this a butterfly soon emerges,
*   flying proudly among the colorful flowers on beautiful wings.*
Mother Nature's performance is steadily and earnestly conducted
*   unlike the actions of those who are lost and who*
*   expend their efforts searching for shortcuts to success.*

Only the one who goes through the specific stages
*   of self-transformation can perfectly attain the betterment of the self.*

One then lives with truth, beauty, and goodness.
But the one who only seeks shortcuts,
   cuts short any benefit and gradually loses life.
Those who expect to be fed by someone else will inevitably end up as the meal.
We should all remember that all lives are born and supported
   by the impetus of Nature, and natural life is found in everyone.

Being gallant can be recognized as a means to survive,
   although it is different in human life.
Being gallant is a noble spiritual quality
   especially when chosen from a moral perspective.

Lao Tzu chose to live among the unenlightened,
   rather than stay in a privileged governmental position and
   support the unhealthy tendency of his time.

Shakyamuni chose to live as a beggar,
   forsaking a life of luxury that was fed by taxes forcefully imposed on the people.
He did not intend to establish any false religion that would go against
   his own spiritual attainment, and he was not responsible for
   the false establishment that came after him.

Jesus chose to challenge the false social establishment of his time
   rather than simply enjoy his truthful attainment.
In his own way, he interpreted the natural truth as:

The Sky (God) is my father.
The Earth (God) is my mother.
All people are my brothers and sisters.
My life seeks to be one with the Way—
   the Great Mother of the Universal Nature.

Jesus was also not responsible for the false religion that came after him.

Mohammed chose to be inspired by the
Way of Universal Spiritual Truth, which has no particular images or names,
   rather than bending his life to the confused idolatry of his time.

He chose the name Ara, known today as Allah,
*   and established the sun as the central image of his new social order.*
Mohammed was not responsible for the dilution of his message
*   that occurred after his time.*

The high attainment of these great spiritual identities
*   may be expressed as follows.*

Lao Tzu: "Moral wisdom takes no advantage of the underdeveloped, but helps them."
Shakyamuni: "The divine soul empties out the self."
Jesus: "Nature and life are closely related as parent and child."
Mohammed: "The truth of the universe is formless, imageless, and nameless."

People who learn from these sages can express the truth in their own lives.

People who learn from Lao Tzu value the moral nature of life above all else.
People who learn from Shakyamuni practice selflessness.
People who learn from Jesus befriend the Sky, the Earth, and all people.
People who learn from Mohammed do not hold onto formality, image, or name,
*   but stay with unity instead.*

In these ways, one can directly experience the natural truth.

The religious establishments that followed those truthful realizations
*   have diluted and altered the sages' original messages,*
*   deviating from the natural truth.*

Living the highest quality of spiritual life means acting gallantly
*   from a clear moral choice that goes beyond considerations of personal safety.*
Divine life is selfless. This is Nature's Way.

When people's conscience sits on the throne of their life,
*   divine consideration receives first priority.*
This is the highest spiritual quality.

I praise the examples of great moral courage given by Lao Tzu,
*   Shakyamuni, Jesus, and Mohammed.*

People who follow their moral motivations
    rather than perpetuating the partial views of the times,
    give a similar example.
They are not confused by people's superstitions,
    the prevailing social forces, or the herding forces of social custom and ritual.
By their behavior, they show that they clearly perceive
    and deeply appreciate the natural spirit of life whereby:

The Sky is my father,
The Earth is my mother,
All people are my brothers and sisters.
With the support and protection of all gods, deities,
    and achieved human ancestors,
    I enjoy living in the heart of the Great Mother of All Universes.

The Universal Mother embraces all ways of personifying God.
The Universal Mother embraces all high truths.
The Universal Mother embraces all divinity, all beauty, and all goodness.

Hail to the Universal Mother who gives birth to all beings as well as all non-beings.
Hail to the Universal Mother who gives birth to all things as well as to nothing.
The void of nothing gives rise to all things.
It is the beginning of all life and natural phenomena.

Hail to the Universal Mother who is the Great Life of all.
You are imbued with the sense of being.
You are the source and origin of all life.

Hail to the Universal Mother
    who gives birth to both divine and ordinary life,
    without seeking reward.

Who else can achieve this?
Most mothers on Earth show the right example.
A dutiful mother carries the virtue of the Universal Mother,
    and she fulfills that virtue on Earth.

Hail to the Universal Mother whose high morality
 is fulfilled by the many mothers on Earth,
 all of whom I respect.

Universal Mother,
You provide us with both a physical form and
 a high level of consciousness that enables us to see ourselves.
Without consciousness, we would be like a worm with a naked body,
 simply eating, sleeping, fighting, and having sex.
The power of consciousness enables us to transcend the level of beasts
 and ascend to your high light.

Our conscious energy can be further developed and become the master of life.
Should we keep riding endlessly on the meaningless treadmill,
 or should we awaken from the lower sphere of cyclic mechanical action?
After many stages and lifetimes, we can become more than an animal without a tail.
All life and matter are but different expressions of Mother Nature,
 among which human life is the closest to Nature.
Those of us who live in harmony with Nature,
 can live with a high consciousness of life and challenge death's authority.

Birds know nothing of higher life,
 and most animals just accept the limitations of their form.
But a being with a high level of consciousness can go beyond these limitations.
In the light of the Universal Mother,
 a true spiritual faith can change our lives.
Even a black crow-like being can transform into a beautiful phoenix.
An enormous dragon can develop from the being of a small snake.
Whoever cultivates the spiritual faith of eternal life
 will learn the simple fact of natural transformation and go beyond.
One firsts need to examine all the limitations that can be false.
Natural limitations, though, may be seen in physical forms
 such as in the process of life and death.
But the natural spiritual potential of humans is complete and free.
After spiritual achievement,
 one can transcend the laws of physical transformation.

Staying in the lower sphere
   of coarseness and roughness is a choice.
Those who do not abuse their life
   can appreciate the opportunity of being human.
There are those, however, who abuse and poison that
   opportunity by busily running after external pursuits.
They lose the vision of what is possible in themselves.
May these people come to appreciate the value of their natural life
   with its innate spiritual potential.
Only then will they be able to spiritually transform.

Being gallant is a clear moral choice.
It can be the highest spiritual quality.
When personal safety is beyond consideration,
   the consciousness of people is imbued with divinity.

Mastery of life may be attained,
   when one gives full attention to one's own humble life.
Death can also be transcended, as a few achieved ones have shown,
   and spiritual achievement may be realized.

Nature is immortal, though its forms are mortal.
Spiritual evolution can be enhanced.
The resolution of soul energy can shape itself differently.

The formed sphere of life has limitations, but the unformed sphere has none.
Though the unformed sphere may receive the influence of life's lower spheres,
   any contamination can be removed and purity restored.
For those who are able to achieve truth, beauty, and goodness,
   there is eternal life.
For those who dwell in the eternal abyss,
   there is only eternal darkness.

Dear Universal Mother,
Through my humble prayer,
   may people awaken to the preciousness of their lives
   that is a divine opportunity to become better and higher.

Dear Mother,
You are the source and origin of all life.
You are within everything, and you are also detached from everything.
You are being, and you are non-being.
You are the object, and you are nothing.
I love you with all my heart.

Down by the seaside, the roar of your waves
    dispels the city noise I carry within.
Your turquoise ocean cleanses my body.
Your swiftly changing weather energizes my vitality.
Your natural world and the helpful kindness of friends
    are an expression of your endless beauty.

Thank you, Mother!

Chapter 32

When the Universal Mother Speaks to Me

When the Universal Mother speaks to me,
    she speaks through the sky, sun, moon, and stars.
She speaks through the Earth, oceans, rivers, lakes, and streams.
And she speaks through the mountains, trees, and meadows.

She speaks to me through all her natural creations.
They all carry her voice.
All of Nature is her utterance.

Each time I stop my busy mind,
    my heart overflows with love for her,
    like water from a mountain spring, pure and clean.

Without a mother's love,
    a child cannot smile and an adult cannot mature.
Mothers are the first to teach love to the lives of the young.
A mother's unconditional love is the foundation of all love.
A mother is the gentle, sweet spirit
    that makes unhappiness and worries disappear.

The world is full of suffering
    because people do not see the true nature of a mother's love.
They lack insight into the interconnectedness of all beings and things.
The all-pervading love of Nature is the inter-beingness
    that connects through and with all.

The beauty of the Hue River embraces and deeply inspires me.
The water of the river, running forever,
    is like my love for the world and its people.
Though this river may live outside of me,
I have a life river inside of me.
Though all beautiful waters impress me,
    they are but the semblance of the river inside of me.

The river that impresses me most deeply is the river of life.
It has no beginning and it will have no end.
It is always there.
So many streams have entered it,
* nourishing and supporting the flow of life.*

The river of life is always transforming.
Although its face may change from time to time,
* its original purpose is always there,*
* providing continuous support to all forms of life to grow and thrive.*
It is the stream of my life to be more than alive.

When I allow my life to be with Nature's vastness,
* I touch deeply each life and each thing I encounter.*
I walk mindfully along the path of life
* and understand the need to help others*
* who are but parts of the one, whole being that is inside and outside of me.*

There is deep compassion and kind love that
* runs forever like the continuous flow of rivers.*
My life speaks from the range of its own being
* through the deep support of the Mother Universe.*

Chapter 33

Live Naturally

(From Auckland, New Zealand)

To the cosmic mother above,
*   to the cosmic mother within,*
*   and to the cosmic mother without,*
*   thank you for providing me with everything.*

You are the Universal Divine Nature within and above all divine beings.
You are the only true ground that supports all created faiths,
*   names, images, and styles of worship.*
You are the real support of all small confidences and beliefs.
You are the great Truth above all.

You are the only divine source; there is nothing above you.
Your universal nature is the only reality.
Because you are the non-created divinity of Nature,
*   you are the most trustworthy and most responsive of all.*

You are the Way.
The Way is straight.
It is people who like to detour.

You are the Way.
The Way is clear.
It is people who like to form mazes.

People have tried to describe you in order to establish their
*   spiritual authority for selfish worldly gain, but this is untruthful.*
The human sense of divinity is an expectation and projection
*   from the immature mind.*
It is a mixed-up idea.

There is nothing beyond you.
You represent the purest.
There is nothing beside you.
You represent wholeness.

You are the divine essence of all divine beings.
You are the deepest knowledge of all branches of knowledge.
You are the most capable of all capabilities.
You are unlimited.
You withdraw from any emphasis on partiality.

I pray for your light.
In your light,
    no one is born evil, nor is anyone permanently evil.
It is the circumstances of a person's life that make them so.
If there were time for them to correct themselves,
    they could change or mend.

The root of people's mistakes is in how they perceive others and the world.
People lose themselves because they lose their spiritual vision
    or fail to develop it.
They misinterpret circumstances and respond incorrectly.
And, since life is short, the opportunity of
    conducting life correctly and uprightly is limited.
Once an evil thing is committed,
    there is usually little or no chance for repair and redemption.
Therefore, we should all heed this serious warning that
    in the conduct of our life we need to be careful.
When faced with a choice between right and wrong,
    we should always choose what is upright and straight, not crooked.

Dear Mother,
The simple Truth is that there is no one who is born specially
    so that they have no need to improve themselves spiritually
    or become spiritually aware.

Though there may be times and situations
   where almost everyone is controlled by a common destiny,
   individual effort can still make a difference,
   and help us to liberate our lives from the common fate of the situation.

However, when we consider the one, big background of life,
   there is still the natural common destiny that is not subject to change,
   wherein all people need to help each other and cooperate together.

Spiritual effort can make a difference in one's life
   by building a better spiritual equality of life.
No one should be considered an absolute authority,
   and be allowed to command over others.
This is the root of human weakness.

The Truth is inside of life, not beside it.
There is no real way to separate the Truth and life.
The Truth is in the correct meaning and performance of life.
Those who live in ways that go against this Truth
   approach the darkness of death.
When can those people see the light?
I pray to your Divine Light for them.

I know that my life is eternal because you are eternal.
Most people fail to develop this opportunity though,
   because they keep searching for worldly treats and privileges.
These people only end up troubling others and hastening their spiritual death.

In your light,
   eternal life is found within people's lives,
   when they conduct their life naturally.
Searching for and desiring more and more,
   only digs a deeper grave.

Whoever goes against the naturalness of life
   shall end their life sooner with an unnatural death.
The darkness of ignorance, stupidity, and evil intent,
   work against the natural intent of a long and happy life.

In your light,
I see that the people of the world as well as the world of people
have made the world more and more difficult.
In this situation, should those of your offspring who are awake
stay away from or stay close to those who are lost?
In your light, I have learned to accept people's differences
and appreciate their varied and positive creations.

Some people grow higher and some remain spiritually dwarfed.
Those who do not grow keep to the limiting framework
that someone set for them a long time ago.
Whether it is their choice or comes from a collective mistake,
how can you help?

I have heard that the same type of grain
can raise hundreds of different types of people.
But in Nature there is no uniformity.
The birds enjoy flying in the sky,
the fish enjoy swimming in the water,
and people live on the land.
There is no need for religious or social uniformity.
The nature of life has no need of unnatural change.

The safety and happiness of the world can be achieved
if everyone would learn to be content and enjoy
the different and varied foods and customs of others.
Without contentment, people become too aggressive
in their search to expand their desires.

Respect for Nature should be a universal practice.
Those who do not respect the naturalness of life are lost.
Specifically, there are three types of people who are lost.
Those who are overly aggressive,
those who are overly externally oriented,
and those who are overly selfish.

These people have shackled their spiritual growth,
preferring to stay in the darkness of their familiar habits.

But just as snakes know how to shed their skin
in the different stages of their growth,
people can break the shackles that obstruct their spiritual growth
by learning more about the naturalness of life.

When we live naturally,
every day, from Sunday to Saturday, is a good day.
Good and evil are only real
when lives are harmed because someone overextended their desires
and preyed upon others.

Dear Mother,
With your light, we can know how to love one another.
With the growth of wisdom,
we can love our lives and the lives of others.
Evil occurs when greed and aggression are overextended.
An early death awaits those who act in such ways,
whereas eternal life will be received by those
who believe in eternal life for all.
Eternal life is your Universal Nature.
It is an opportunity offered to everyone.

Dear Mother,
You are the root of Life and Nature, thus
I expect to live close to your life as much as possible.
You are the Mother of Nature and the Mother of everlasting life.
You are the source of the pure essence of all beings and things.

With you,
Life is Beautiful.
Life is Truthful.
Life is Light.
Life is Wisdom, and
Life is Universal Divinity.
I dedicate the highest essence of my life
to be your shrine.

With my deepest gratitude I say:
You are the Mother Nature of the Universe.
You are the Universal Mother of Eternal Life.
You are the Mother of All.

Thank you,
Great Mother of All Universes.

Chapter 34

Know the Subtle Law

(From Beachaven, New Zealand)

Great Mother of the Universe,
   thank you for bringing me here.
As I gaze quietly over the peaceful harbor,
   I see the tide is gentle and the yachts are still.
The sun shines on a bridge full of flowing cars.
The gentle tide moves me deeply inside to reflect on matters of humanity.

Although humans are but a tiny life, they can be extremely arrogant
   when it comes to defending their mistakes.
As they ignorantly build their culture and proclaim supremacy over all,
   they neglect and compete intensely with the facts of Nature.
How narrow and self-important they make themselves!

Nature gives birth to all things.
From her base, higher beings and higher lives can develop.
Humans, who are endowed with higher consciousness and intuition,
   should be able to recognize and admit that before Nature
   there was no being that could be known by the mind;
   there were no gods before Nature's birth.
Thus, although we can have the ambition to explore,
   allowing that ambition to become assertive
   about what our minds cannot truly know
   shows a lack of growth.

The concept that Nature is created and controlled by a superior being
   is based completely on self-assertion.
People who think that this is so reflect the smallness of their own minds
   rather than the natural reality.

Many generations of social leaders have attempted to order society
   by creating governments and religions.

But because such attempts have been based on a fraud,
   and are far from the natural reality,
   many societies have arisen and fallen.
In particular, to assert that the sky
   is the real source of power over people is fraudulent.
And if human culture is based on fraud, what is its real destiny?

Once a society designs a social order and a plan is put into place,
   force and fraudulence are often applied to ensure its acceptance by all.
Yet, surely it is reasonable for the highest form of life
   not to demand that everything be shaped as their mind desires.
Nature and the nature of life are to be understood, not controlled.

Too much control only ends
   in the destruction of Nature and society.
It certainly causes damage to the natural harmony, balance,
   and happiness of life.

Far better that human society follows the natural order of life,
   as this is how family naturally develops.
The mind may assist in this natural process,
   provided we do not disturb or interfere with the normal,
   organic growth of life and society.

It is best to learn to simply accept the nature of the Universe,
   and respect the subtle nature of all things.
Although the nature of the mind is one of these subtle things,
   we should also respect the fact that what is unknowable
   is the Mother of all that is knowable.

People who do not understand or respect the principles of Nature
   become too ambitious.
Religions have been created to satisfy the need for order.
Many of these ruling systems forced people to accept
   that the most powerful source of order came from the sky.
However, those who initiated religions were not really clear about that source
   since they were lacking in spiritual depth and achievement.

Generally, everyone has a spiritual nature.
However, most need spiritual guidance
  in order to help them appreciate that nature
  and support its growth.
Because of this need, many have been misguided
  by the small and cunning minds of religious leaders
  whose teachings, rather than being based on the
  universal spiritual reality of Nature,
  were developed to fit a particular race and circumstance.

All lives are the children of Mother Nature,
  and Nature comes from nothing.
In terms of the human mind,
  there is nothing which can be created from nothing,
  although it is possible that something could be
  restructured to form a new creation.
Even modern technology illustrates that science
  is the work of discovery, not creation.
Mother Nature is the exception.
Born from nothing she becomes something.
She is the model of self-development,
  and within her innate development lies the natural subtle law.

The universal subtle law governs
  the interplay of nothing and something.
It can be recognized in the unfolding
  nature and play of the Universe.

Each new generation needs a constructive direction and
  a healthy social order for its optimum survival.
This is a very serious matter,
  and no one should ever again presuppose
  the spiritual source of any new order.
Although human rationality can be a good source of understanding,
  this is only so if people have carefully studied the universal subtle law
  with its principle of yin and yang.
This is the law of Nature, not some human law.

The subtle law shows that what is overly positive
  will soon turn to be negative,
  and that the discovery of a negative force
  is an opportunity for correction.
The subtle law balances itself,
  and therefore people must find their own balance
  in everything they do.

The subtle law shows that a real ruler is no ruler.
The ruler who is no ruler and the rules which are no rules
  can only be sketched like this:
The universal virtues of unity, harmony, symmetry, and balance
  are the real rulers and real rules of life
  and of Nature herself.

Once the true ruler is recognized,
  each person is able to conduct their life peacefully and cooperatively,
  which has a positive effect on the ordering of society at large.
The old framework of established societies
  can be a real obstacle to the new global effort,
  but less damage can be created if we take a balanced approach.

We should all see clearly and know
  that the life of Nature is expressed in cycles and rhythms.
For example, each cell in a human body is renewed every seven years.
This force of renewal comes from Mother Nature.
Learning how to renew ourselves is the only way to everlasting life.
Only Mother Nature knows how to renew herself,
  thus she is everlasting.
We must all learn renewal from her.

Nature is the big life,
  while people are its small models or offspring.
All small lives share in the big model of Nature.
Old conventions teach there is one True Lord, God.
In the Integral Way, however,
  we recognize that that True Lord or God is Mother Nature.

Mother Nature inspires those who achieve
  the depth and clarity of their spiritual nature
  to teach others how to order their lives spiritually.

All sages, prophets, messengers, or awakened ones
  have but one heart and one spiritual motivation—
  to restore natural spiritual and social order
  to the world and people's lives.
This aspiration is reflected in their own lives.
There is nothing more important.
Such effort must continue for the survival and positive progress of humanity.
We all need to know how to naturally manage
  our internal life and the external social order.

Mother Nature may be perceived by many images and called by many names,
  but truly there is nothing that goes beyond her source
  even when we consider the concept of the supernatural.
Even if such phenomena exist, they must have come from Mother Nature
  otherwise they could not exist or are not real.

We humans invent frameworks for our convenience and easy perception,
  but if there is a super nature it must be the subtle sphere of Mother Nature.
If we define what we can see, hear, touch, taste, smell, and measure
  to be the forms of Nature,
  then that which is unable to be seen, heard, touched, tasted, smelled,
  and measured must be what is known as the supernatural.
Whether formed or unformed, each is a different sphere of the one Mother Nature.

Our conceptual ability enables us to conceive of any image the mind can create.
This includes the numerous cultural and spiritual beliefs and customs
  that reflect different human mentalities.
Though there is no need to unify the many different expressions,
  there is a need for a common spiritual understanding of the foundation of life
  whether in the physical or spiritual sphere.

All positive and healthy cultural fashions should be preserved,
  as everybody has their own rate of growth and need to choose.

However, it is important to be aware that our
   personal faith and beliefs affect the destiny of our lives.
Therefore, the basis of a better and higher life
   lies in a common, universal spiritual faith and understanding of life,
   and the qualities of receptivity, open-mindedness, and rationality.

Once a universal common faith is clear,
   a common destiny can be recognized
   and conflicts between different styles can be dissolved.
Spiritual reflection can help in this endeavor
   since those with deeper spiritual development
   find it easier to accept differences.

The True Lord is Mother Nature,
   and her subtle law is the only reality.
Mother Nature can be known through personal growth and development.
The mind is the vehicle that carries the conscious energy from Mother Nature.
In fact, knowledge of her universal subtle law shows development of the mind.
Although her subtle network seems like mesh,
   nothing can escape its operation.
The performance of the subtle law is Mother Nature's exercise.
This natural movement pattern is the True Lord of my life and yours.
It is my fate and yours.

Examples of Nature's two spheres are:
Male and female,
Apparent and hidden,
Physical and supernatural,
Expansion and contraction,
Giving and receiving,
Aggression and yielding.

And it is the harmonious interaction of the two spheres that gives rise to unity.
The simplest expression of this subtle Truth is: ☯
This symbol expresses that there is duality in unity,
   and that in every natural unity there is duality.
This understanding comes from the intuition of those individuals
   who have reached the deep truth in their seeking.

Dear Mother,
Your universal subtle law is the True Lord and fate of all lives.
Please allow your sons and daughters,
who have been confused by many names,
descriptions, and images, to return to you.
The basic truth should now be recognized
that the universal reality is beyond the powers of description and illustration.

Dear Mother,
Forgive all of us who competed with you
by creating religions through our limited minds.
Today, religion is used as a psychological weapon
to prepare people for physical war.
But it is our ignorance about the subtle law
that is the key problem limiting our survival.

We know nothing of your profound tolerance towards us.
If you become impatient, all is lost.
Your tolerance should be the only true religion.
With this understanding, all difficulties can be resolved.

When we do not nurture the nature of life,
which is about expressing love and kindness to all,
then even the smallest amount of negative emotion
can develop into an unfathomable abyss,
drowning all involved.

Mercy is a great power.
Use it to pardon small mistakes and to teach people
how to avoid the big mistakes of humanity too.

Dear Mother,
The untruth is supported by clouds of continued darkness.
The truth was first supported by the strength of one person, the Yellow Emperor.
Now his descendants, my family, the Ni family,
along with our many ancestors and sincere friends,
continue to live the truth.

My sons and I, with the support of our family,
   have created a university that teaches the Integral Way,
   the goal of which is to offer a true and complete education
   about the subtle Reality to everyone.
In order to build support and make the teachings widely available,
   we founded the Integral Way Society (IWS)
   and the Path of Constructive Life (PCL).

Dear Mother,
By your grace we exercise our lives to convey
   the understanding of the natural truth to all lives.

Chapter 35

Embrace Unity

(From southern New Zealand)

Most Respectful Mother of the Cosmos,
*   you are the Mother of all.*
You embrace all things and all beings in your heart.
All things and all beings are but the physical expressions of your formlessness,
*   and all things and all beings are but the segmented expressions*
*   of your subtle essence.*
Through them, you express the supreme beingness of Nature.

It is a predicament that the human mind distorts the truth.
My work, as your small child,
*   is to restore confidence in the plain, true Nature of life.*

When people invented language,
*   an abundance of stories arose describing the origin of life.*
These were mostly created during the stage
*   when people's imagination had overgrown their perception,*
*   so few people could see the Integral Truth as the nature of the Universe*
*   because all descriptions are partial*
*   due to the limitations of the narrative mind.*

The Way was thus chosen to convey the image of the subtle reality.
While the Subtle Origin is always sketched reluctantly,
*   it still carries the genuineness of the Way.*

As the Way is described,
*   the unlimited gives birth to the limited,*
*   and the limited supplements the unlimited.*

The creative force of the non-created Original Nature
*   brings forth all creatures and creations,*
*   and they reveal the non-created Origin.*

The life that can be classified by gender
  is but the offspring of the One that has no gender.

The things and beings that can be known by form
  are formed by the One that has no form.

It is through an open, pure, and inclusive perception
  that such visions and intuitions of Nature's reality can be received.

In the beginning of natural life,
  there was no pre-existing mastermind or great creator of life.
These are but human concepts superimposed
  over the natural pattern and movement of life.
While the ecological balance of the natural world is often seen as Nature's function,
  if people would cast their gaze wider they would see
  that the operation of Nature's subtle law is behind everything,
  including one's individual life and all of human history.
Developing the wisdom to see this is more important
  than any concept about creation.

The great law and principle of yin and yang
  expresses the basic pattern of natural movement—
  its rhythms, cycles, and alternations.
These principles, recorded in the I Ching,
  are achievements from the intuitive power of highly conscious lives,
  while modern physics uses new terminology
  merely to supplement those principles with similar discoveries.
Modern physicists expect to put all the segments together
  to see the big picture or unified whole,
  but this only satisfies the intellectual mind.
If you wish for a description from modern research,
  you can study the theory of quantum physics.

It is far more important that people discover the universal subtle law
  in order to manage their own lives.
If human history is earnestly and correctly recorded,
  it shows evidence for the existence of such a Law
  that relates to all laws.

Human society is small, and individual human lives are even smaller.
Yet, each carries the reflection of Nature because like mother, like child.
The universal subtle law can be found
in the center of each and every being and thing.

No matter whether a life is big or small,
its misfortune and unhappiness expresses a disharmony with the subtle law.
Whoever or whatever goes against this law will soon cease to exist.

The law of Nature is the same as the law of life.
Conscious energy is a subtle form of Nature's power.
It is also the subtle essence of life.
Nature extends this conscious power to the higher life of humanity
in order that people can govern themselves.
But people often misuse their consciousness in ways
that destroy the harmony between their lives and the subtle law.

Polarization is the tendency in all movement,
whereas unity, balance, and equilibrium is the power of everlasting life.
The world and all lives are activated by the impetus of Nature
and thus share in its tendency to move towards extremes.
While the natural force is installed within everything,
only the higher form of human life
is given the power of consciousness
to save itself and share in life's sovereignty.
Although a life is able to receive the force of Nature,
it can erroneously transform that force into emotion
and end up competing with the nature of life.
Those who use Nature's life force impulsively
without seeking for internal unity and external balance
usually end up ruining themselves or their society.

No sage or hero can help a life that loses its
unity or balance through extremes.
This is why Lao Tzu makes the comment that
the sky, Earth, leaders, and all people have a unity,
but once that unity is lost, they lose their existence.

Lao Tzu also teaches the importance of cultivating the Way
  in order to gain and maintain self-unity.
Once gained, the Way, as the ultimate Truth or Unity is also there.

Chapter 36

Follow the Light

(From a place one step to Heaven)

Dear Universal Mother,
Thank you for providing us with the natural inspiration
  of the source of life on this planet, Earth.

The ocean is the mother of humankind
  and water is the blood of the Earth.
When the sun sends out its light,
  the light and water interplay
  and the deep ocean conceives life.

When the human mind deviates from this Nature
  with its stories and metaphors about creation,
  it misleads people.
In depth, it is the mystical force between the light of the sun
  and the water of the ocean that has brought forth human life.
The rays of the sun heats the water to become vapor
  from which countless tiny spiritual lives are conceived.
Invisible and immeasurable, these spirits
  are the foundation of the larger, fleshly forms of life.
Although relatively immortal, these tiny lives
  still comply with the natural law of constant transformation.

During the death of the fleshly form,
  the tiny spiritual components are released back to the sky.
It was from the partial experience of the spirits
  that the early religious leaders inaccurately shaped
  the different images of God.

All lives carry a certain amount of conscious energy,
  which is the functioning part of most lives.

With experience of the depth of life,
  we come to understand that both the conscious energy
  and the natural spiritual particles compose life.
When these energies converge, they form life
  and when they separate, the form of life ceases to be.
However, there is one important exception:
When the tiny spirits of Nature become strong,
  they can converge together to become a natural force or appear in some form.
People may not recognize this spiritual convergence
  or have an accurate image of it,
  because the spirits may not form in a way that the mind demands.

The soul of a human is the remaining conscious content of one's life experience
  which stays together with those tiny spiritual entities
  that come from the original level of the natural substance of life.
That subtle union in an individual life may last for awhile.
Upon the death of the fleshed life,
  the tiny soul usually adheres to the blood relations.
In the end, it may become a newly fleshed life or be scattered away.

Divine souls are those souls that are perfectly in tune with the natural Law.
This can occur when the soul inhabiting the human form
  lives in accordance with the subtle law.
In people's lives, though, it is the mind that is usually accepted
  as their counselor, not the subtle law.
The human mind contains the highest conscious energy
  among all the fleshed forms.
However, it needs further development
  since the spiritual sphere needs to be taken care of
  so it can become more than the physical sphere
  and low desires of human life.

In Nature, there are two types of high energies.
Both are natural spiritual energy but with different characteristics.
In all human life,
  the mind carries the yin type of spiritual energy,
  which is the conscious energy,

and the body carries the yang *type of spiritual energy,*
  which are the numerous bodily spirits of life.
The body spirits can form themselves and be felt
  by individuals and small groups of people.
When presented alone,
  they may appear as physical matter or spirits.
When they converge at the spiritual level,
  they produce a spiritual light called pure yang.

The mind is also yang *because of its more active nature,*
  while the conscious energy is yin *because of its hidden, latent nature.*
This is an example of yin *within* yang,
  as well as an expression of yang *embracing* yin.
The physical form of life is yang *because it is apparent,*
  whereas the body spirits are yin *because they are latent.*
This is an example of yang *within* yin,
  as well as an expression of yin *embracing* yang.

Some early, developed individuals hid the discovery of these energies
  and their relationships within the symbol of the T'ai Chi.

T'ai Chi means the Ultimate Truth of Nature.
It has two sides—a white force and a black force
  that express the embrace of yin *and* yang.
There is a small, white spot in the black domain,
  which shows the lesser yang *in the major* yin.
And there is a small, black spot in the white domain,
  which shows the lesser yin *in the major* yang.

In Nature, there is constant change and transformation.
Neither yin *nor* yang *remains the same.*
When the lesser yin *grows in the major* yang,
  the yang *can be replaced if its negative aspect is overly strong*
  as this helps the growth of the yin.
When the lesser yang *grows in the major* yin,
  the yin *can be wiped out*
  if the positive strength of the yang *increases.*

Naturally, when the yin increases, the yang decreases,
  and when the yang increases, the yin decreases.
This natural dance is the alternating steps of advancing and retreating.
Its rhythm is not hard to see, particularly in human society.

In the life of an individual or of society,
  one cannot expect things not to change.
The issue is not really about change,
  but how one copes with change.
To help in this endeavor, three books should be thoroughly studied:
The I Ching *gives the formula of lasting normality,*
  the Yellow Emperor's Classic[1] *guides you*
  on how to naturally care for your life,
  and the Tao Teh Ching, *or* Book of Universal Morality,
  teaches the wise way to accommodate Nature.

Dear Universal Mother,
Some of us think that you are far from our earthly life,
  yet your universal nature is right here, giving birth to us all.
The sun is one of your outposts and messengers
  that vitalizes this branch of your Nature with our human life.

Millions, if not billions of years ago,
  basic life appeared on Earth
  carrying with it the potential of human life.
From that early time and up to the present,
  that life potential of humanity has evolved and learned many things.
Yet most of that knowledge relates to physical things.
Spiritually, most minds live in the same darkness they have always lived in.
They follow leaders who make up stories about the world
  that contort the natural spiritual sphere
  and who fuel wars with their conceptual weapons.

---

1. See Dr. Maoshing Ni's version of *The Yellow Emperor's Classic* entitled *The Yellow Emperor's Classic of Medicine*, Shambala Publications, 1995.

Ignoring the truth that is as apparent as the light
  and following establishments that are attached to the dark
  is self-deceiving.
There is no stupidity greater than this.

Emotional dependence is often the push
  that causes people to turn to religion,
  but it was often political motives that led to their initial creation.
Interdependence is the truth of life,
  and a healthy emotion can be a positive force
  when guided towards the natural Truth.

The image of the sun once served
  as the symbol of social leadership,
  and although this has not been so for some time,
  the sun's support remains unchanged.
It is we who have lost the vision to see the plain and simple truth
  of our relationship with the sun.
The sun is the messenger of the Universal Mother.
The sun's light is her love given to all life.

We should accept the plain truth that life is natural
  and develop our life from this very basis.
No one is born divine,
  but the way we conduct our lives can help us to become so.

Have confidence in Nature.
Respect its natural life.
With experience, the wisdom of our life can grow
  and with continuous cultivation comes the promise
  of higher development and achievement.
Humankind can achieve itself through each individual's
  sincere effort to harmonize with the natural environment.

Dear Universal Mother,
We are lost in a cultural fog of our own creation.
Help us blow away the clouds with your gentle breeze.

Help each of us see the reality of our life
  which is rooted in Nature,
  rather than rooted in our own conceptual creation and confusion.

Chapter 37

Clear Away the Mental Fog

(From Perth, Australia)

Dear Mother Universe,
You are both the Mother of all lives and things,
*   and the Nature in all lives and things.*
This basic foundation is the same for everyone.

Although we are all your children,
*   many of us are unable to recognize your support and care.*
Instead, we have created many stories, beliefs, and images,
*   that only confuse ourselves and others.*
We have become so proud of our foolish indulgences.

Most of what we call holy, sacred, and sublime
*   only reflects our deviation from the natural truth.*
Moreover, most people insist that their fiction
*   is the highest truth above all.*
This type of farce continues generation after generation,
*   and is often played out in wasteful war.*
This is wrong.

Great Mother of the Universe,
*   the human mind has fallen into a thick fog of its own creation.*
This has been so for around 3,000 years.
People's eyes have been heavily clogged,
*   their ears have been deafened,*
*   and their tongues have grown forks and thorns.*
Most of their creations come
*   from the imagination and illusion of their confused minds,*
*   none of which can replace your plain and subtle reality.*

The mind is the tool to help us live honestly and respectfully.
It should not be used to deviate from the simple natural truth.
People have created and dreamed up different heavens and
   different authorities to rule over the truth of their natural life.
Many thick books were written in people's dreams
   which they insist are the only truth.
But only you, Mother Nature, are not a fiction;
   you are not created by the mischievous human mind.
Nothing is more truthful than you.

Dear Mother of the Universe,
Your children have fallen asleep
   causing us to become lost
   in the thick jungle of our own cultural creation.
Help us to clean ourselves inside and out.
Help us to restore the joy of our natural life.
Allow those of us who are lost to return to you.

Dear Mother,
We may have been unruly.
We may have been ignorant, mischievous, and foolish.
Now we stand on the edge of razing our earthly home.
Please wake us up to see the real danger we face.

With utmost sincerity, we beseech your pardon.
Please accept your sons and daughters back into your heart
   where we can enjoy and share in your eternal life.
Help us to retrace back before the creation of sounds, images, and words,
   back to your Holy Womb—the real Subtle Origin—
   where there are no sounds, forms, or words,
   only the wordless ultimate Reality.

The simple essence you endow in our lives is the most valuable.
From it we are able to create, recreate, and find new opportunity.
Help us learn over again the value of this simple essence in our lives
   rather than waste our energy in emotional fantasy.

Help us learn to value our existence
  and to become aware enough not to add anything to it
  so as not to create any emotional cancer,
  financial cancer, political cancer,
  or the cancer of over-establishment or religious manipulation.

Enable our conscious power to be used in ways
  that prevent our precious existence
  from being devoured by our negative trends.
And allow all of us to learn to protect our healthy life nature
  with the highest respect.

Chapter 38

Be Tao

Mother Nature holds all lives in her boundless heart,
   while the spiritual growth of my life becomes the eyes that see myself in her.
The timeless homeland is the permanent residence of my true life.
My true life is ageless since it knows to constantly renew itself
   by living endlessly with her rhythmic pace.
Yet, it also knows it has been assigned to evolve higher.

Mother Nature teaches her offspring with the wordless truth
   that is clearly expressed everywhere in everything
   to a mind that is not obstructed.
No words are needed and no book can contain it.
In other words, the formless origin of all formed lives and things
   can be reached through unobstructed vision.
It lies far beyond all the doors and names
   that have been created by the human mind.
No matter how clever our mind is,
   it always confuses itself by chasing its own tail.
Through clear spiritual vision, I am able to see
   the wordless truth contained in my life's simplicity
   that needs no emotional or conceptual declaration.
The original simplicity of each person's life
   is the most direct expression of the wordless truth.
The true being of my life therefore embodies the life of the Universe.
Where else do I expect to find divinity?

As the true essence of universal life,
   my life resides always in the timeless homeland
   where there is no artificial division between past, present or future.
As the true essence of universal life,
   I experience the unlimited reality in which I live as the Universe.
My life is a universal life in a time capsule, yet it can expand to universal enormity.
My true life never departs from the timeless homeland,
   although it visits the world from time to time and goes from place to place.

Some people believe that ageless life exists separately from other lives.
Others believe that the wordless truth is not to be found in ordinary life.
This may indeed be the truth of their lives
   due to their narrow conceptual choices,
   but it serves them negatively.

It is true that the physical form is limited and therefore ages.
Chi *is also limited and can be scattered.*
Universal life is unreachable by the mind
   which can only comprehend things of limitation.

The being of Tao has no limitation.
Tao is beyond conception.
Yet, it can also be physical, and it can be chi.
Tao can be all things, but it is not limited
   by the partial definitions assigned to it by the mind.

Tao is the Integral Truth.
It is above all lives and, at the same time, within all lives
   that do not forsake their true nature.
Tao does not rely on anything, even though it is related to all things.
Tao can be with itself, even though it has no self.
Where or what then is Tao?
It lies within the naturalness and balance of each life
   and the normal order of all things.

Tao is within my life.
Tao is outside my life.
Tao is my physical body.
Tao is my chi.
Tao is my mind.
Tao is my soul.
Tao is full of me.
I am full of Tao.
Tao is the subtle essence of Universal life.
Tao is the subtle essence of my life.
But, Tao cannot be known by a life lacking in spiritual development.

Tao is nothing.
From nothing comes something, and something becomes nothing.
Yet, nothing cannot always remain nothing so it becomes something again.

Does my life ride on Tao?
Or is it Tao that takes a ride on me?
What really matters is knowing
  whether there is any separation between my life and Tao.

All things and lives appear by taking a free ride on Nature's wheel.
As the wheel turns, different cycles appear.
Riding high on the wheel,
  one tends to become overly aggressive and proud.
Riding low on the wheel,
  one tends to hold on tightly and become sour towards the outside world.
Embracing Tao, one knows the wheel is not external
  so one chooses to live a balanced life that is not overly internal or overly external.
Such a person does not fall.

Tao is the free ride of life.
Tao is the wheel of Nature.
Tao is Nature.
Tao is the subtle law of Nature.
Tao is the subtle essence of life.
Things and lives come and go, but Tao does not come and go.
Tao is eternal.
Tao is never tired of being.
True life is Tao, thus our life—yours and mine—is eternal.

In worldly life, what limits your everlasting life?
It is your lack of spiritual growth.
In worldly life, what causes your far-reaching life to shrink so small?
It is the obstructions in your mind that set limits on your growth.
Do you judge Tao by setting racial boundaries?
Do you limit Tao by worshipping a sacred image?
Do you lose sight of Tao by focusing on the past history of your race?
Do you neglect the true wholeness, the Integral Truth,
  by being self-obsessed?

Most people pursue the development of tools
*   that only serve the physical aspect of life.*
They forget the goal of life itself.
The public is taught that technology is the glory of their lives.
This is the greatest human ignorance.

Truly, the Integral Truth is the natural truth of all lives.
No false salvation can replace it.
The one who lives with the Integral Truth finds true life
*   which includes all time, all space, and all people.*

The Integral Truth serves not just one person but all people.
It serves not just one race but all races.
It serves not just one kind but all kinds.
It serves not just one time or place but all times and all places.

Tao stands for:
   T   the truth
   A   above
   O   ourselves

   T   the truth
   A   among
   O   ourselves

This reality is not for philosophical discussion.
It is the subtle energy or life energy of the Universe.
Everyone is a part of that life energy.
Once you understand this,
*   you will not object to this new word,* Tao.

PART VI

Inspirational Readings

Diamonds do not grow in haystacks.
They grow from the extreme pressure of heat and cold.
A soft life is easy to enjoy and makes me sleepy.
A challenging life keeps me awake to bring forth
my incorruptible diamond personality.

Chapter 39

The Universal Mother's Blessing

The Mother of the Universe gives birth to all the galaxies.
The galaxies give birth to all the solar systems.
Our solar system is but one of many.

Human life is the convergence of all of the best energies in the universe.
This deep relationship with the entire Universe is a precious gift.

Each person's life is a wonderful opportunity for sublimation.
This gift, which is the inherent nature of the universe,
   is nothing less than the gift of ultimate freedom.

The universal flow in which all lives swim
   has only one direction.
It is like riding a raft in a swift current through a deep ravine.
We must go forward or be swallowed by the waves
   and diminished by the rocks.

Chapter 40

Prayer to the One and Only Lord

Among all human creations,
   none is the True Lord or Lady of life.
Only the simple essence in all life
   is the True Lord.

From the simple essence is born
   the balanced mind and universal heart.
These are the highest expressions
   of health in human life.
These are also the only message
   that ever comes from the True Lord of Life.
This message is what connects all sublime souls
   in the embrace of Boundless Divine Light.

The good nature of most people,
   the health and normality of most life,
   contains such simple truth, above any verbal distortion
   that its beauty is evidence of the only True Lord.

To live is to embrace divine light.
Purity, uprightness and wisdom are testimony
   to the simple but most profound truth of life.
None of the thick books in any human language
   compare to this.

The soul that is upright, pure and wise,
   with the power to realize goodness and health
   is able to breakthrough any darkness,
   and give the birth to the everlasting oneness of
   Universal Divine Light.

Chapter 41

A Good Life Versus a Good Heart

If we have a good life and a good heart,
   we can enjoy a long and happy life.

If we have a good life but a bad heart,
   our blessings can turn into suffering.

If we have a good heart but a poor life,
   our troubles and suffering can change into blessings.

If we have a poor life and a bad heart,
   we will surely meet with trouble,
      which could end in an early death.

A good heart can save our life.
There is no secret to this.
We simply need to be kind.

The condition of our life is created by the condition of our heart.
A good heart is able to invite good fortune,
   and reverse a negative situation.

Mere faith in pursuing good fortune, however,
   without the support of a good heart,
      usually ends in misfortune.

Let us cultivate our hearts,
   while looking to Nature to be the True Lord of our lives.
Heaven and Earth will then naturally protect us.

Those of us who understand that
   it is we ourselves who create our life's fortune, whether good or bad,
      are able to maintain and cultivate our blessings.
A good heart is the key.

Chapter 42

Ode to a Constructive Life

身是生命樹，
心是日月光，
吾生長向陽，
根莖花果堅.

My body is the Tree of Life,
    its mental core the light of the Sun and Moon.
Throughout a lifetime facing the light,
    its root, trunk, flowers, and fruit become hardy and complete.

身是生命樹，
心是日月光，
吾生永向陽，
生氣自然旺.

My body is the Tree of Life,
    its mental core the light of the Sun and Moon.
Life ever facing the light,
    it naturally glows with the spark of life.

身是生命樹，
心是日月光，
吾生永向陽，
人生自發皇.

My body is the Tree of Life,
    its mental core the light of the Sun and Moon.
Life ever facing the light,
    maintains endless growth.

吾生存純朴，
原始之至眞，
與生而具存，
抱陽愼勿失．

My life retains its pure nature,
  the profound truth of its Source.
Keep to it forever.
Embrace the light. Ensure it is never lost.

吾生存淳樸，
原始未失眞，
隨生而俱來，
敬保愼毋失．

My life retains its pure essence; its simple candor,
  most essential, never lost to life's changes.
With birth comes life's truthful integrity.
Nurture it with respect. Take care never to let it slip despite life's changes.

一日之計在乎晨，
一年之計在乎春，
一生之計在乎勤，
莫等閒白了少年頭．

Each day is counted from the dawn.
Each year is counted from the spring.
Each life is accounted for in diligence.
Waste not in idleness the flower of youth.

Chapter 43

Uniting Our Diamond Personality with Tao

During my younger years, my parents taught me the following verses as part of my spiritual training. They encouraged me to recite them throughout my life. Using them as I have will help you to uplift and balance your emotions.

I

Homage to the Way of Everlasting Life:
The Truth About Oneself.
The Truth Above Oneself.
The Truth Among Ourselves
   and the trinity of all three.

Homage to the Way of Everlasting Life:
Tao gives birth to the One.
The One gives birth to two—the unformed and the formed.
The two jointly give birth to a third,
   which is between the formed and the unformed.
There are thus three gems in the universe.
These do not exist independently of one another,
   but remain an interdependent whole.

Homage to the Triple Gem:
Heaven, Earth, and Humankind which evolved from Nature.
Together, these three—the unformed spiritual sphere,
   the formed material sphere, and the middle sphere called life,
   uphold the great being of Universal Oneness.

I offer these verses in praise of the Universal Subtle Origin,
   which is prior to all natural creation and is known as
   the Giver of Goodness,

the Lord of Transcendent Happiness,
and the Master of Wholeness and Health.
It underlies all high achievement as the simplest Nothingness.

Goodness is produced from all points of view
because the nature of life itself is good.
Goodness is the invisible nature of the universe.

I offer these verses in praise of the Invincible One,
the Unaffected One.
All beings who hear me will be freed from bondage,
just as I will be.

I I

O' Seer of the World,
when your great wisdom merges with our good hearts,
all defilement will be cleansed.

All human life contains the three gems,
each of which has its own function
and accomplishes its own purpose in an individual's life.
But the Triple Gem is the true victor.
Any projection of a single gem,
without the support of the other two, cannot last.

Let me hold fast to the Victor
who wins the great "non-retailed" victory.
Let me strive for liberation from a partial view.

Come, come wise teachings, come to me.
Come through me and spread universally.
Having conquered the lower sphere and fear of death,
enlightenment comes to the one
who is open to the universal Truth.

O' Merciful One,
 when you encourage my terrified mind to be strong
 and transcend all partiality,
 I accomplish greatness in my life.

To cultivate the Accomplishing Power of Sincerity,
 I must be able to bravely break through all obstacles.

I I I

Homage to the Triple Gem
 of the formed material world,
 the unformed spiritual reality,
 and the life sphere between the two.

Homage to the holy Oneness.
May my wishes be accomplished,
 and may I free myself from bondage and purify my life
 with my pure hands and kind heart.

O' Seer, who through calmness attains the
 radiant splendor of wisdom
 and transcends the world while living within it,
 I admire and bow to you.
Come forth my own awakening wisdom
 so that I may appreciate the wholeness of my being.

Descend all help, descend!
Inspire me to eliminate all contamination and conscious defilement.
Destroy death and temper evil so that my mind and heart
 may be grounded in the Earth, and inspired by the galaxies and stars.
Through wholeness of being I reach the subtle, invisible reality.

I am willing to work at breaking through darkness.
I am willing to work at uplifting the world from trouble.
I cherish such victory and will be victorious.

I V

The oneness of Nature brings forth the Triple Gem of my life,
  and with it the wholeness of unadorned virtue.
I turn away from, dispel, and annihilate
  any desires and passions that are unbalanced.
I strive to surpass what is good and refrain from what is bad.
I nurture goals that are constructive and pure,
  both in myself and other people.

The Invincible One whose power is gentle, subtle, and ever persistent,
  exists invisibly among all beings.
Homage to all who see the subtle truth.
They exclaim "Hurrah!" for the victory of virtue.

V

Adoration to the one who possesses the Triple Gem
  of an enlightened mind, a universal heart,
  and sublimated passion.

Homage to the one whose nature is whole,
  and whose unobstructed vision can clearly see
  the problems of the world.
The deep awakening of such a one
  can safely avert others from the traps of life.

Homage to the one who respects
  the immanent nonexistence above all existence,
  the nonbeing of Tao among all beings.
With great compassion,
  such a one bestows love and respect to all.

Homage to the one who is able to make
  the great leap beyond all fear!
Homage to the one who protects others from danger
  without broadcasting their accomplishment.

Such a one praises the Giver of All Good,
    the Doer of All Good, and the Maker of All Good.

Having not merely adored the Great One,
    may I enter the heart of the most Noble and Loving One
    whose life completes all meaning.
Such a one's purity makes all beings victorious,
    and cleanses their path of existence.

Happiness belongs to the one who masters life.
Happiness is never achieved by those who accept life as a slavish burden.

Homage to the one who possesses the greatness
    to bring, convey, and offer all that is good and positive to life.
For such a one has severed and destroyed all negativity within oneself.

V I

The Great Victor abides with
    the virtue of the sky, the virtue of the Earth,
    and the completeness of a human being.
She is equal-minded towards all.
Her freedom is unlimited.
Her heart is pure.
Her soul is immaculate.
Her spirit is unmarred.

Liberation is the mark of her being.
She comes with goodness.
She subdues the black serpent.
She wears the protective armor of the constructive, centermost Way.
She has great joy springing up from within.
She continues the life of wisdom.

She destroys all poisons in her life
    and teaches others about:

The poison of luxury,
   which can lead one to deviate from the true nature of life;
The poison of meaningless attachment;
The poison of foolish ambition to grasp the world,
   which only leads to insanity, and
The poisons of anger, hatred, and prejudice,
   which spoil the world and make life difficult.
All of these need to be cleansed and overcome.

May I overcome the beast of desire.
May my wisdom grow from worldly life
   like the lotus flower that rises above the murky pond.
May I refresh my life, and may my newly empowered life
   rise up and be received!

VII

Descend high wisdom!
Come down enlightenment!
Enter me bright knowledge!
Come, all of you!

Awaken me!
Enlighten me!
Inspire me!

I am the life of balance between
   the pressure of the formed,
     and the uplifting reality of the unformed.
I dare to seek and speak wisdom.
My heart is so glad to attain the wisdom
   that develops from my terrified, small mind.

Hurrah! Hurrah! Hurrah!
   to the successful one,
     to the accomplished one.

Homage to the one who has attained mastery through self-discipline,
  and who does not rely on false images
  created for undeveloped people.

Homage to the accomplished one of self-concentration,
  who lays life's trifles under one's feet.
Homage to the one of great freedom.

V I I I

Hurrah! Hurrah! Hurrah!
To the one who unifies the two spheres
  of the formed life and the unformed spiritual reality within oneself.

Hail to the destroyer of the lazy swine
  sleeping in the mud of inertia.
Hail to the lion tamer of selfish desire.
Hail to the invisible sword of wisdom.
Hail to all the great accomplished ones,
  who enjoy purity of hand and mind.

The victor of the outer world
  wins only half the victory.
The victor of spiritual difficulty
  wins the victory deep within the soul.
Yet, complete victory belongs only to the one
  who embraces Universal Oneness.

I X

Great is the one who is triumphant over outer difficulties.
Greater still is the one who is triumphant over inner difficulties.
Greatest is the one who is triumphant over one's own tension,
  which demands so much of one's life energy.

Great is the one who is able to avoid worldly trouble.
Greater still is the one who is able to avoid making trouble for oneself.
Greatest is the one who is able to dissolve trouble
   before it happens to oneself or others.

Wise is the one who does not fall into the traps of others.
Wiser still is the one who does not to fall into the traps
   of one's own emotions or hasty decisions.
Wisest is the one who has no greed for more, for better,
   or for greater advantage in any situation.

The great fortune is to eliminate misery, sorrow,
   and sadness from one's life.
The greater fortune is to eliminate misery, sorrow,
   and sadness from one's surroundings.
The greatest fortune is to be able to save the world
   without creating new trouble.

Great is the one who does not make trouble for oneself.
Greater still is the one who does not make trouble for others.
Greatest is the one who does not achieve personal ambition
   at the expense of another.

Cheers to the one who activates the cosmic spirit.
Cheers to the one who turns the wheels of one's own life.
Cheers to the one who opens the hidden channels
   in the body and mind, and who knows how to stop the leaks.
Cheers to the one who can be enlightened
   by a simple, natural voice and sound,
   who has no need of elaborate works,
   and who is not confused by shrewd and clever tongues.
Cheers to the one who enjoys the purity of life
   as if it were a lotus flower rising above the murky water.
Cheers to the far cause of my complete life.

X

Hurrah!
To the victory of being whole.
Hurrah!
To the beneficent one
   whose vision encompasses the beginning of the universe.
Hurrah!
To the many people of universal conscience,
   who help sow the seeds of goodness.
Hurrah!
To the one of great simplicity,
   who carries the deep truth of constructive existence.
Hurrah!
To the invisible one of gentle, subtle, and enduring power
   on my left, on my right, and in my middle.
Hurrah!
To the one who frightens those cruel wolves in sheep's clothing.

Adoration to my Spiritual Treasure.
Adoration to the Achieved One.
Adoration to the one who frees one's life from all obstacles.
Adoration to the one of great freedom.

Hail to the one of all-accomplishing.
Hail to this magnificent chant
   which guides me to live the Integral Way.
Hail to my personal life which unites with Tao—
   the indivisible whole and power of natural consciousness.

Diamonds do not grow in haystacks.
They grow from the extreme pressure of heat and cold.
A soft life is easy to enjoy and makes me sleepy.
A challenging life keeps me awake to bring forth
   my incorruptible diamond personality.

Chapter 44

Ceremony for Rejuvenation

(This practice is suitable for individual and group gatherings.)

I bow to the Way.
The Way is the nature of the universe.
The Way is the nature of all life.
The Way is the nature of my life.

I bow to the Way.
The Way is constantly rejuvenating.
The Way rejuvenates the universe.
The Way rejuvenates all life.
The Way rejuvenates my life.

I bow to the Nature of the Universe.
Rejuvenation is the truth of the nature of the universe.
Rejuvenation is the truth of all life.

I bow to the Way.
The Way is the truth about my life.
The Way is the truth above my life.
The Way is the truth among all lives.

I bow to the Way.
The Way is the Mother of the Universe.
The Way is the Mother of Life.
The Way is the Mother of Truth.

I bow to the Way.
The Way gives life to One.
One gives life to two.
Two gives life to three.
Three gives life to all.

I bow to the Way.
The Way is the nature of the universe.
Its normal flow is gentleness.
Gentleness gives birth to life
My life continues with gentleness.

I bow to the Way.
The Way is constructive and enduring,
   whereas violence is self-limiting,
   which is why it cannot last long.
Though violence brings destruction,
   it is also a tool for renewal.
It prepares the way for newer and better constructions of life.
But the short-lived phenomenon of subnormal forces
   can never replace the normal, constructive
   and enduring flow of the universe.

I bow to the Way.
The Way is unified.
Wise people embrace the unity of the Way.
They do not show off nor try to justify their lives.
They distinguish their lives by maintaining a natural, normal life,
   not by bragging or receiving recognition.
By simply being who they are,
   they brighten the world and set an example for all.

I bow to the Way.
The Way is the highest.
Those that achieve it are generally not known
   because they appear so normal among lives.

I bow to the Way.
The highest among us lives with the universal normality.
Between normality and subnormality
I know what to love, fear, and despise.

I bow to the Way.
The Way is constant.

I know who and what to trust.
I trust the normality of the constant nature of the universe.

I bow to the Way.
The Way is sacred. I cannot demand it.
Those who try to bully it will destroy their life.
Those who try to hold it will lose their life.

I bow to the Way.
The Way is in the front, rear, and middle.
The Way is everywhere.
But people miss seeing it in the normality of their everyday lives.

I bow to the Way.
The Way appears nonexistent because of its plain normality.
Yet people are troubled by loss and yell as a result of pain.
They seem to respect negativity and subnormality,
    and ignore the all-important normality that supports their lives.

I bow to the Way.
The Way is normal,
    yet most people are excited by the subnormal.
They even address it with high titles and exalt it to be divine.
Some create statues for it and bow to these daily.
I alone adore the formless normality.

I bow to the Way.
Most people worship the fear that has been transformed
    from the negativity and subnormality, and which is exalted to be divine.
However, all the names created for such a divinity
    share in the one reality of human fear.

I bow to the Way.
The different names people create arouse competition among themselves
    even though these all come from the same reality of fear.
I alone adore the Way.
The Way is the normality that no life can miss in any second.
I call it no other name but the Way.

I bow to the Way.
Most people hold onto fear
    as their spiritual motivation
    and name it God.
I alone pay attention to the normality of each proceeding moment.
Thus, I am at ease with grace.

I bow to the Way.
The Way is flavorless, plain, and simple.
Because the Way is plain and simple,
    no one is interested in enjoying it!
No one celebrates normality.
People prefer to be excited by troubles,
    which they reexperience through celebrations.
They even make merry—eating and drinking out of fear.
They eventually live for the fear of troubles
    in order to witness what they consider to be the power of the divine.
As a simple being, I alone know to enjoy the
    flavorless, plain, and simple normality in each passing moment.

I bow to the Way.
When people create concepts and make things
    in order to serve the fear of losing their life,
    they actually make their life suffer more
    for the burden of their unnecessary creations.

I bow to the Way.
I do not neglect it or do it too often.
Rather, I follow the normality of life of which most others tire.
I alone take nourishment from those "boring and tiresome"
    yet precious passing moments,
    in which there is no negativity and subnormality
    to overshadow the power of my life.

I bow to the Way.
How do I serve the Way?
The Way is in the front, rear, and middle.
People do not see it because it is just there.

Seeing it they become excited,
   which only makes it disappear.

I bow to the Way.
By serving the Way I may disappoint others
   because my life proceeds normally
   without extremes, indulgence, or complacency.

I bow to the Way.
When I am strong, I do not use my good strength to overcome others.
When I am weak, I enjoy the softness and do not try to strengthen it
   in order to match or compete with my surroundings.

I bow to the Way.
Understanding comes when I live
   without creating disturbances or relying on stimulants.
Realizing the simple truth of life by living so plainly
   is to have gained understanding.
One of deep realization influences their surroundings with peace,
   and is less affected by the flow of worldly events.

I bow to the Way.
Fear can cause a life to behave subnormally.
For example, when afraid, dogs' bark and wild animals become violent.
Living normally requires spiritual power.

I bow to the Way.
Most popular religions are based on fear and are therefore subnormal.
Tyranny exists due to the fear of the people.
Democracy exists due to the fear of a ruler.
Most worldly establishments are based on fear.
I live with the simple and fearless Way.
Fearlessness is achieved by attaining absolute spiritual unity.

I bow to the Way.
At a time when the world considers the subnormal as normal,
   what can I do?

Do not be afraid as fear cannot conquer fear;
   it only leads to more trouble.
The Way is to live calmly until the Way is appreciated.

I bow to the Way.
Haste makes my mind tense and panic spoils my life.
Both lead to my inappropriate reactions.
But by giving my life some space and quiet,
   my inner spiritual health can function by itself,
   helping me to be aware of the conditions
   that cause my tension and inappropriateness.
There is no need to go far in search of sages.

I bow to the Way.
I bow to the truth about my life.
I bow to the truth above my life.
I bow to the truth among all lives.
I bow to the truth of the Universal One Truth.

Chapter 45

The Way

I stay with the Way.

To be Nothing is to be whole.
To be something is to be partial.
To be Nothing is to be with the wholeness of all things.
The omni-presence is therefore Nothing.

To be something is not complete or long-lasting.
To be something is the limited life of all things.

To embrace Nothing is to embrace all things.
To hold something, including a holy name or established worship,
    is to hold what is partial and limited.
All holy names such as God, Allah or Buddha
    are mere projections from the Way of Integral Infinity.

The Way cannot be held onto or insisted upon.
Whatever can be held onto is not the Way of the whole truth.

This is the Way.

INDEX

TEACHINGS OF THE INTEGRAL WAY BY THE NI FAMILY

The Path of Constructive Life: Embracing Heaven's Heart—Unveils the new vehicle of the Integral Way known as the Path of Constructive Life. It gives fresh direction and effective self-practices to achieve sexual harmony, emotional well-being, protection from harmful influences and a universal soul.
#BHEART—315 pages, softcover. $19.95

The Power of the Feminine: Using Feminine Energy to Heal the World's Spiritual Problems—The wise vision of the feminine approach is the true foundation of human civilization and spiritual growth. When positive feminine virtues are usurped in favor of masculine strength, violence and aggressive competition result, leading the world to destruction. In this book, Hua-Ching Ni and Maoshing Ni touch on how and why this imbalance occurs, and deeply encourage women to apply their gentle feminine virtue to balance masculine strength and reset the course of humanity.
#BFEM—270 pages, softcover. $16.95

The New Universal Morality: How to Find God in Modern Times—An in-depth look at living in accord with universal virtue; particularly relevant with the disappointing failures of conventional religious teachings and the degraded condition of modern morality. Authors Hua-Ching Ni and Maoshing Ni Ph.D. reveal a natural religion in which universal morality is the essence, the true God that supports our lives and all existence. A direct discussion of the nature of God and the process of becoming a spiritual coach to serve both our community and ourselves.
#BMOR—280 pages, softcover. $16.95

The Majestic Domain of the Universal Heart—By Hua-Ching Ni and Maoshing Ni Ph.D. This book examines the power of universal love and wisdom and shows you how to integrate these life forces into your life through deepened spiritual awareness. In addition to drawing from the teachings of Lao Tzu and Chen Tuan, Hua-Ching Ni offers his own inspiring guidance for all who are seeking spiritual growth through an integral way of life.
#BMAJ—115 pages, softcover. $17.95

The Centermost Way—Hua-Ching Ni has written an inspiring account of human spiritual development, from its earliest stages, through the course of the last two millennia, up to today. It is a guidebook for those seeking a way of life that includes family, work, social activities and interests, scientific and religious pursuits, art, politics, and every other aspect of existence that we know and experience in the course of a lifetime on earth.
#BCENT—181 pages. $17.95

Enrich Your Life With Virtue—By Hua-Ching Ni. By embracing a life of natural virtue, one reduces conflict in the world. However humble this may seem, its personal spiritual and social implications are far-reaching. By examining the history of human relationships from this perspective, Hua-Ching Ni offers a broad study of human nature and draws on a centuries old tradition of natural life that transcends cultural and religious difference.

#BENR—173 pages. $15.95

Foundation of a Happy Life—By Hua-Ching Ni. A wonderful tool for making spiritual life a part of everyday life through instructive readings that families can share together. The future of the human world lies in its children. If parents raise their children well, the world will have a brighter future. A simple family shrine or alter, and regular gatherings to read the wisdom and advice of spiritually achieved people, can contribute profoundly to the development of strong characters and happiness.

#BFOUN—190 pages. $15.95

Secrets of Longevity: Hundreds of Ways to Live to be 100—By Dr. Maoshing Ni, Ph.D. Looking to live a longer, happier, healthier life? Try eating more blueberries, telling the truth, and saying no to undue burdens. Dr. Mao brings together simple and unusual ways to live longer.

#BLON—320 pages, softcover. $14.95
Published by Chronicle Books

Strength From Movement: Cultivating Chi—By Hua-Ching Ni, Daoshing Ni, and Maoshing Ni. *Chi*, the vital power of life, can be developed and cultivated within yourself to help support your health and your happy life. This book gives the deep reality of different useful forms of *chi* exercise and why certain types are more beneficial for certain types of people. Included are samples of several popular exercises.

#BSTRE—256 pages, softcover with 42 photographs. $17.95

Internal Alchemy: The Natural Way to Immortality—Ancient spiritually achieved ones used alchemical terminology metaphorically to disguise personal internal energy transformation. This book offers prescriptions that help sublimate your energy.

#BALCH—288 pages, softcover. $17.95

The Time Is Now for a Better Life and a Better World—The purpose of achievement is on one hand to serve individual self-preservation and also to exercise one's attainment from spiritual cultivation to help others. It is expected to save the difficulties of the time, to prepare ourselves to create a bright future for the human race, and to overcome our modern day spiritual dilemma by conjoint effort.

#BTIME—136 pages, softcover. $10.95

The Way, the Truth, and the Light—This is the story of the first sage who introduced the way to the world. The life of this young sage links the spiritual achievement of East and West, and demonstrates the great spiritual virtue of his love to all people.

#BLIGP—232 pages, softcover. $14.95
#BLIGH—Hardcover. $22.95

Life and Teaching of Two Immortals, Volume 1: Kou Hong—Master Kou Hong, who was an achieved Master, a healer in Traditional Chinese Medicine, and a specialist in the art of refining medicines, was born in 363 A.D. He laid the foundation of later cultural development in China.

#BLIF1—176 pages, softcover. $12.95

Life and Teaching of Two Immortals, Volume 2: Chen Tuan—The second emperor of the Sung Dynasty entitled Master Chen Tuan "Master of Supernatural Truth." Hua-Ching Ni describes his life and cultivation and gives in-depth commentaries that provide teaching and insight into the achievement of this highly respected Master.

#BLIF2—192 pages, softcover. $12.95

Esoteric Tao Teh Ching—*Tao Teh Ching* expresses the highest efficiency of life and can be applied in many levels of worldly and spiritual life. This previously unreleased edition discusses instruction for spiritual practices in every day life, which includes important in-depth techniques for spiritual benefit.

#BESOT—192 pages, softcover. $13.95

The Uncharted Voyage Toward the Subtle Light—Spiritual life in the world today has become a confusing mixture of dying traditions and radical novelties. People who earnestly and sincerely seek something more than just a way to fit into the complexities of a modern structure that does not support true self-development, often find themselves spiritually struggling. This book provides a profound understanding and insight into the underlying heart of all paths of spiritual growth, the subtle origin, and the eternal truth of one universal life.

#BVOY—424 pages, softcover. $19.95

Golden Message, A Guide to Spiritual Life with Self-Study Program for Learning the Integral Way—This volume begins with a traditional treatise by Daoshing and Maoshing Ni about the broad nature of spiritual learning and its application for human life. It is followed by a message from Hua-Ching Ni. An outline of the Spiritual Self-Study Program and Correspondence Course of the College of Tao is included.

#BGOLD—160 pages, softcover. $11.95

Mysticism: Empowering the Spirit Within—For more than 8000 years, mystical knowledge has been passed down by sages. Hua-Ching Ni introduces spiritual knowledge of the developed ones, which does not use the senses, or machines like scientific knowledge, yet can know both the entirety of the universe and the spirits.

#BMYSM—200 pages, softcover. $13.95

Ageless Counsel for Modern Life—These sixty-four writings, originally illustrative commentaries on the *I Ching*, are meaningful and useful spiritual guidance on various topics to enrich your life. Hua-Ching Ni's delightful poetry and some teachings of esoteric Taoism can be found here as well.

#BAGE—256 pages, softcover. $15.95

The Mystical Universal Mother—An understanding of both masculine and feminine energies are crucial to understanding oneself, in particular for people moving to higher spiritual evolution. Hua-Ching Ni focuses upon the feminine through the examples of some ancient and modern women.

#BMYST—240 pages, softcover. $14.95

Harmony, The Art of Life—Harmony occurs when two different things find the point at which they can link together. Hua-Ching Ni shares valuable spiritual understanding and insight about the ability to bring harmony within one's own self, one's relationships and the world.

#BHAR—208 pages, softcover. $16.95

Moonlight in the Dark Night—The difficulty for many people in developing their spirituality is not that they are not moral or spiritual enough, but they are captive to their emotions. This book contains wisdom on how to guide emotions. It also includes simple guidance on how to balance love relationships so your life may be smoother and happier and your spiritual growth more effective.

#BMOON—168 pages, softcover. $12.95

Attune Your Body with Dao-In—The ancients discovered that Dao-In exercises solved problems of stagnant energy, increased their health, and lengthened their years. The exercises are also used as practical support for cultivation and higher achievements of spiritual immortality.

#BDAOI—144 pages, softcover. $16.95
Also on VHS & DVD. $24.95

The Key to Good Fortune: Refining Your Spirit (Revised)—"Straighten your Way" (*Tai Shan Kan Yin Pien*) and "The Silent Way of Blessing" (*Yin Chi Wen*) are the main guidance for a mature, healthy life. Spiritual improvement can be an integral part of realizing a Heavenly life on earth.
#BKEY—135 pages, softcover. $17.95

Eternal Light—Hua-Ching Ni presents the life and teachings of his father, Grandmaster Ni, Yo San, who was a spiritually achieved person, healer and teacher, and a source of inspiration to Master Ni. Deeper teachings and insights for living a spiritual life and higher achievement.
#BETER—208 pages, softcover. $14.95

Quest of Soul—Hua-Ching Ni addresses many concepts about the soul such as saving the soul, improving the soul's quality, the free soul, what happens at death, and the universal soul. He guides and inspires the reader into deeper self-knowledge and to move forward to increase personal happiness and spiritual depth.
#BQUES—152 pages, softcover. $11.95

Nurture Your Spirits—Hua-Ching Ni breaks some spiritual prohibitions and presents the spiritual truth he has studied and proven. This truth may help you develop and nurture your own spirits, which are the truthful internal foundation of your life being.
#BNURT—176 pages, softcover. $12.95

Power of Natural Healing—Hua-Ching Ni discusses the natural capability of self-healing, information, and practices which can assist any treatment method and presents methods of cultivation which promote a healthy life, longevity, and spiritual achievement.
#BHEAL—143 pages, softcover. $14.95

Essence of Universal Spirituality—In this volume, as an open-minded learner and achieved teacher of universal spirituality, Hua-Ching Ni examines and discusses all levels and topics of religious and spiritual teaching to help you understand the ultimate truth and enjoy the achievement of all religions without becoming confused by them.
#BESSE—304 pages, softcover. $19.95

Guide to Inner Light—Drawing inspiration from the experience of the ancient ones, modern people looking for the true source and meaning of life can find great teachings to direct and benefit them. The invaluable ancient development can teach us to reach the attainable spiritual truth and point the way to the inner Light.
#BGUID—192 pages, softcover. $12.95

Stepping Stones for Spiritual Success—In this volume, Hua-Ching Ni has taken the best of the traditional teachings and put them into contemporary language to make them more relevant to our time, culture, and lives.

#BSTEP—160 pages, softcover. $12.95

The Complete Works of Lao Tzu—The *Tao Teh Ching* is one of the most widely translated and cherished works of literature. Its timeless wisdom provides a bridge to the subtle spiritual truth and aids harmonious and peaceful living. Also included is the *Hua Hu Ching*, a later work of Lao Tzu, which was lost to the general public for a thousand years.

#BCOMP—212 pages, softcover. $13.95

I Ching, The Book of Changes and the Unchanging Truth—The legendary classic *I Ching* is recognized as the first written book of wisdom. Leaders and sages throughout history have consulted it as a trusted advisor, which reveals the appropriate action in any circumstance. Includes over 200 pages of background material on natural energy cycles, instruction, and commentaries.

#BBOOK—669 pages, hardcover. $35.00

The Story of Two Kingdoms—This volume is the metaphoric tale of the conflict between the Kingdoms of Light and Darkness. Through this unique story, Hua-Ching Ni transmits esoteric teachings of Taoism that have been carefully guarded secrets for over 5,000 years. This book is for those who are serious in achieving high spiritual goals.

#BSTOR—223 pages, hardcover. $14.00

The Way of Integral Life—This book includes practical and applicable suggestions for daily life, philosophical thought, esoteric insight and guidelines for those aspiring to serve the world. The ancient sages' achievement can assist the growth of your own wisdom and balanced, reasonable life.

#BWAYP—320 pages, softcover. $14.00
#BWAYH—Hardcover. $20.00

Enlightenment: Mother of Spiritual Independence—The inspiring story and teachings of Master Hui Neng, the father of Zen Buddhism and Sixth Patriarch of the Buddhist tradition, highlight this volume. Hui Neng was a person of ordinary birth, intellectually unsophisticated, who achieved himself to become a spiritual leader.

#BENLP—264 pages, softcover. $12.50
#BENLH—Hardcover. $22.00

The Gentle Path of Spiritual Progress—This book offers a glimpse into the dialogues between a master and his students. In a relaxed, open manner, Hua-Ching Ni explains to his students the fundamental practices that are the keys to experiencing enlightenment in everyday life.

#BGENT—290 pages, softcover. $12.95

Spiritual Messages from a Buffalo Rider, A Man of Tao—Our buffalo nature rides on us, whereas an achieved person rides the buffalo. Hua-Ching Ni gives much helpful knowledge to those who are interested in improving their lives and deepening their cultivation so they too can develop beyond their mundane beings.

#BSPIR—242 pages, softcover. $12.95

8,000 Years of Wisdom, Volume I and II—This two-volume set contains a wealth of practical, down-to-earth advice given by Hua-Ching Ni over a five-year period. Drawing on his training in Traditional Chinese Medicine, Herbology, and Acupuncture, Hua-Ching Ni gives candid answers to questions on many topics.

  #BWIS1—Vol. I: (Revised edition)
                Includes dietary guidance; 236 pages, softcover. $18.50
  #BWIS2—Vol. II: Includes sex and pregnancy guidance; 241 pages, softcover. $18.50

Footsteps of the Mystical Child—This book poses and answers such questions as, "What is a soul? What is wisdom? What is spiritual evolution?" to enable readers to open themselves to new realms of understanding and personal growth. Includes true examples about people's internal and external struggles on the path of self-development and spiritual evolution.

#BFOOT—166 pages, softcover. $9.50

Workbook for Spiritual Development—This material summarizes thousands of years of traditional teachings and little known practices for spiritual development. There are sections on ancient invocations, natural celibacy and postures for energy channeling. Hua-Ching Ni explains basic attitudes and knowledge that supports spiritual practice.

#BWORK—240 pages, softcover. $14.95

The Taoist Inner View of the Universe—Hua-Ching Ni has given all the opportunity to know the vast achievement of the ancient unspoiled mind and its transpiercing vision. This book offers a glimpse of the inner world and immortal realm known to achieved ones and makes it understandable for students aspiring to a more complete life.

#BTAOI—218 pages, softcover. $16.95

Tao, the Subtle Universal Law—Most people are unaware that their thoughts and behavior evoke responses from the invisible net of universal energy. To lead a good stable life is to be aware of the universal subtle law in every moment of our lives. This book presents practical methods that have been successfully used for centuries to accomplish this.

#BTAOS—208 pages, softcover. $12.95

Concourse of All Spiritual Paths—All religions, in spite of their surface differences, in their essence return to the great oneness. Hua-Ching Ni looks at what traditional religions offer us today and suggest how to go beyond differences to discover the depth of universal truth.

#BCONC—184 pages, softcover. $15.95

From Diversity to Unity: Return to the One Spiritual Source—This book encourages individuals to go beyond the theological boundary to rediscover their own spiritual nature with guidance offered by Hua-Ching Ni from his personal achievement, exploration, and self-cultivation. This work can help people unlock the spiritual treasures of the universe and light the way to a life of internal and external harmony and fulfillment.

#BDIV—200 pages, softcover. $15.95

Spring Thunder: Awaken the Hibernating Power of Life—Humans need to be periodically awakened from a spiritual hibernation in which the awareness of life's reality is deeply forgotten. To awaken your deep inner life, this book offers the practice of Natural Meditation, the enlightening teachings of Yen Shi, and Hua-Ching Ni's New Year Message.

#BTHUN—168 pages, softcover. $12.95

Internal Growth Through Tao—In this volume, Hua-Ching Ni teaches about the more subtle, much deeper aspects of life. He also points out the confusion caused by some spiritual teachings and encourages students to cultivate internal growth.

#BINTE—208 pages, softcover. $13.95

The Yellow Emperor's Classic of Medicine—By Maoshing Ni, Ph.D. The *Neijing* is one of the most important classics of Taoism, as well as the highest authority on traditional Chinese medicine. Written in the form of a discourse between Yellow Emperor and his ministers, this book contains a wealth of knowledge on holistic medicine and how human life can attune itself to receive natural support.

#BYELL—316 pages, softcover. $24.95
Published by Shambala Publications, Inc.

The Eight Treasures: Energy Enhancement Exercise—By Maoshing Ni, Ph.D. The Eight Treasures is an ancient system of energy enhancing movements based on the natural motion of the universe. It can be practiced by anyone at any fitness level, is non-impact, simple to do, and appropriate for all ages. It is recommended that this book be used with its companion videotape or DVD.
#BEIGH—208 pages, softcover. $17.95
Also on VHS & DVD. $24.95

The Gate to Infinity—People who have learned spiritually through years without real progress will be thoroughly guided by the important discourse in this book. Hua-Ching Ni also explains Natural Meditation. Editors recommend that all serious spiritual students who wish to increase their spiritual potency read this one.
#BGATE—316 pages, softcover. $13.95

Entering the Tao—Traditional stories and teachings of the ancient masters and personal experiences impart the wisdom of Taoism, the Integral Way. Spiritual self-cultivation, self-reliance, spiritual self-protection, emotional balance, do's and don'ts for a healthy lifestyle, sleeping and dreaming, diet, boredom, fun, sex and marriage.
#BENT—153 pages, softcover. $13.00
Published by Shambala Publications, Inc.

The Tao of Nutrition—By Maoshing Ni, Ph.D. with Cathy McNease, B.S., M.H. Learn how to take control of your health with good eating. Over 100 common foods are discussed with their energetic properties and therapeutic functions listed. Food remedies for numerous common ailments are also presented.
#BTAON—214 pages, softcover. $14.95

Revealing the Tao Teh Ching: In-Depth Commentaries on an Ancient Classic—By Xuezhi Hu. Unique, detailed, and practical commentaries on methods of spiritual cultivation as metaphorically described by Lao Tzu in the *Tao Teh Ching*.
#BREV—240 pages, softcover. $19.95
Published by Ageless Classics Press

Chinese Herbology Made Easy—By Maoshing Ni, Ph.D. This text provides an overview of Oriental Medical theory, in-depth descriptions of each herb category, over 300 black and white photographs, extensive tables of individual herbs for easy reference and an index of pharmaceutical names.
#BHERB—202 pages, softcover. $18.95

101 Vegetarian Delights—By Lily Chuang and Cathy McNease. A lovely cookbook with recipes as tasty as they are healthy. Features multicultural recipes, appendices on Chinese herbs and edible flowers, and a glossary of special foods. Over 40 illustrations.
#B101—176 pages, softcover. $15.95

Chinese Vegetarian Delights—By Lily Chuang. An extraordinary collection of recipes based on principles of traditional Chinese nutrition. Meat, sugar, dairy products, and fried foods are excluded.

#BVEG—104 pages, softcover. $7.50

The Power of Positive Living—By Hua-Ching Ni. Ideas about simple improvements and changes in attitude that can be made in everyday life to increase our positive energy and health. Attain real internal peace while attaining external success and security.

#BPOWE—65 pages, softcover booklet. $8.50

Self-Reliance and Constructive Change—By Hua-Ching Ni. Being attached to cultural and religious fashions can hinder personal health. Hua-Ching Ni presents the Integral Way of spiritual discovery that is independent of cultural, political or religious concepts.

#BSELF—54 pages, softcover booklet. $7.00

The Universal Path of Natural Life—By Hua-Ching Ni. Study the ancient spiritual practices of *Yin Fu Ching*, a predecessor of the *Tao Teh Ching*. Connect with the natural unity and balance of the universe to nurture our spiritual essence and natural vitality.

#BPATH—109 pages, softcover booklet. $9.50

POCKET BOOKLETS & MISCELLANEOUS

Progress Along the Way: Life, Service and Realization—The guiding power of human life is the association between the developed mind and the achieved soul, which contains love, rationality, conscience, and everlasting value.

#PPROG—64 pages, paperback. $4.00

The Light of All Stars Illuminates the Way—Through generations of searching, various achieved ones found the best application of the Way in their lives. This booklet contains their discovery.

#PSTAR—48 pages, paperback. $4.00

The Heavenly Way—"Straighten Your Way" (*Tai Shan Kan Yin Pien*) and "The Silent Way of Blessing" (*Yin Chi Wen*) are the main sources of inspiration for this booklet that sets the cornerstone for a mature, healthy life.

#BHEAV—42 pages, softcover. $2.50

VIDEOTAPES & DVDS

Harmony T'ai Chi Short Form (DVD)—By Maoshing Ni, Ph.D. Easy to learn 18 steps *t'ai chi*. Simplified from the regular 108-step T'ai Chi Chuan Parts I & II Harmony Style Form. Graceful movements for balance, peace and vitality.
#DSTEP—DVD, 28 minutes. $24.95

T'ai Chi Sword Form (DVD)—By Maoshing Ni, Ph.D. A short, instructional 10-minute sword form to help sweep away emotional obstacles and enhance protective energy. Excellent for developing spiritual focus.
#DSWORD—DVD, 19 minutes. $24.95

Crane Style Chi Gong (VHS, PAL & DVD)—By Daoshing Ni, Ph.D. Crane Style standing exercises integrate movement, mental imagery and breathing techniques, and are practiced for healing purposes. They were developed by ancient Taoists to increase energy and metabolism, relieve stress and tension, improve mental clarity, and restore general wellbeing. We are thrilled to also offer a reshoot on DVD of this incredibly beautiful old classic.
#VCRAN—VHS video, 120 minutes. $24.95
#VPCRAN—PAL video, 120 minutes. $24.95
#DCRAN—DVD, 120 minutes. $24.95

Attune Your Body with Dao-In (VHS, PAL & DVD)—By Hua-Ching Ni. The ancient Taoist predecessor to T'ai Chi Chuan. Performed sitting and lying down, these moves clear stagnant energy. Includes meditations and massage for a complete integral fitness program.
#VDAOI—VHS video, 60 minutes. $24.95
#VPDAOI—PAL video, 60 minutes. $24.95
#DDAOI—DVD, 60 minutes. $24.95

Taoist Eight Treasures (VHS, PAL & DVD)—By Maoshing Ni, Ph.D. Unique to the Ni family, this 32-movement *chi* form opens blocks in your energy flow and strengthens your vitality. Combines stretching, toning, and energy conducting exercises with deep breathing.
#VEIGH—VHS video, 46 minutes. $24.95
#VPEIGH—PAL video, 46 minutes. $24.95
#DEIGH—DVD, 46 minutes. $24.95
#DEIGHOriginal—DVD, 120 minutes. $24.95

T'ai Chi Chuan, An Appreciation (VHS)—By Hua-Ching Ni "Gentle Path," "Sky Journey," and "Infinite Expansion" are three Taoist esoteric styles handed down by highly achieved masters and are shown in an uninterrupted format. Not an instructional video.

#VAPPR—VHS video, 30 minutes. $24.95

T'ai Chi Chuan, Parts I & II (VHS & PAL)—By Maoshing Ni, Ph.D. This Taoist style, called the style of Harmony, is a distillation of the Yang, Chen, and Wu styles. It integrates physical movement with energy and helps promote longevity and self-cultivation.

#VTAI1, #VTAI2—VHS videos, 60 minutes each. $24.95
#VPTAI1, #VPTAI2—PAL videos, 60 minutes each. $24.95

Self-Healing Chi Gong (VHS, PAL & DVD)—By Maoshing Ni, Ph.D. Strengthen your own self-healing powers. These effective mind-body exercises strengthen and balance each of your five major organ systems. Two hours of practical demonstrations and information lectures.

#VSHCG—VHS video, 120 minutes. $24.95
#VPSHCG—PAL video, 120 minutes. $24.95
#DSHCG—DVD, 120 minutes. $24.95

Cosmic Tour Ba-Gua (VHS, PAL & DVD)—By Hua-Ching Ni. Cosmic Tour Ba-Gua has healing powers similar to T'ai Chi, but the energy flow is quite different. Ba-Gua consists of a special kind of walking which corrects the imbalance and disorder of "having a head heavier than the rest of the body."

#VCOSM—VHS video. $24.95
#VPCOSM—PAL video. $24.95
#DCOSM—DVD. $24.95

T'ai Chi Chuan: The Gentle Path (VHS)—By Hua-Ching Ni. The movements of *The Gentle Path T'ai Chi* guide us to follow the gentle, cyclical motion of the universe. By gathering energy in the lower *tan tien*, the root center, the movements will change our internal energy and guide us to a peaceful and balanced life.

#VGENP—VHS video. $24.95

COMPACT DISCS

Tao Teh Ching—This classic work of Lao Tzu has been recorded in this two-disc set that is a companion to the book translated by Hua-Ching Ni. Professionally recorded and read by Robert Rudelson.

#CDTAO—104 minutes. $15.95

Invocations for Health, Longevity and Healing a Broken Heart—By Maoshing Ni, Ph.D. "Thinking is louder than thunder." This cassette guides you through a series of invocations to channel and conduct your own healing energy and vital force.

#CDINVO—30 minutes. $12.95

Pain Management with Chi Gong—By Maoshing Ni, Ph.D. Using visualization and deep breathing techniques, this cassette offers methods for overcoming pain by invigorating your energy flow and unblocking obstructions that cause pain.

#CDPAIN—30 minutes. $12.95

Meditation for Stress Release—Dr. Mao's breath/mind exercises help us counter the ill effects of our stress filled lives by awakening our protective healing mechanisms. Learn to calm your mind and restore your spirit with ten minutes of simple meditation practices.

#CDSTRESS—30 minutes. $10.95

The Five Clouds Meditation—With James Tuggle. Three important practices from the Shrine Ceremony of the Eternal Breath of Tao and the Integral Way of Life. Beginning with a guided relaxation to increase your receptivity, you are then guided through the five energy systems and related organs to help thoroughly cleanse and balance your internal energy. It ends by refining your energy through the deeply potent Golden Light Meditation and Invocation.

#CD5CLOUDS—60 minutes. $12.95

Meditations to Live to Be 100—By Maoshing Ni, Ph.D. This two-disc set includes cleansing, rejuvenating, and harmonizing meditations for fueling yourself with vital universal *chi* and for living a longer, richer and more satisfying life.

#CDLON—120 minutes. $19.95
Published by Sounds True, Inc.

BOOKS IN SPANISH

Tao Teh Ching—*En Espanol.*
#BTEHS—112 pages, softcover booklet. $8.95

THE INTEGRAL WAY BOOKS, DVDs AND CDs

The books, DVDs and CDs of the Integral Way are published by Tao of Wellness Press, an imprint of SevenStar Communications. If you would like to find out more about us, order a catalog, or place an order for books or other items, please contact us at:

Telephone: 1-800-578-9526
Website: http://www.sevenstarcom.com
E-mail: taostar@taostar.com

SPIRITUAL STUDY THROUGH THE COLLEGE OF TAO

The College of Tao was formally established in California in the 1970s, yet the tradition from which it originated represents centuries of spiritual growth. The College values the spiritual development of each individual and offers a healthy spiritual education to all people.

The College of Tao is a school without walls. Human society is its classroom. Your own life is the class you attend; thus students grow from their own lives and from studying the guidance of the Integral Way.

Distance learning programs, based on the writings of Hua-Ching Ni and his family, are available for those who do not live near an Integral Way of Life center. For more information, visit http://www.taostudies.com or http://www.sevenstarcom.com. For further information and updates on correspondence courses being offered, please contact: info@taostudies.com. For regular mail, please contact the College of Tao at: 3362-141 Street, Surrey, B.C., Canada V4P 3L7.

It is recommended that all Mentors of the Integral Way use the self-study program to educate themselves. Anyone who wishes to teach the practices contained in Hua-Ching Ni's books must apply to the College for certification.

INTEGRAL WAY SOCIETY (IWS, formerly USIW)

❑ I wish to receive a list of registered Mentors teaching in my area or country.

❑ I am interested in joining/forming a study group in my area.

❑ I am interested in becoming a Mentor of the IWS.

❑ I am interested in subscribing to the IWS quarterly newsletter.

Name: _____

Address: _____

City: _____ State: _____ Zip: _____

E-Mail Address: _____

Mail this request to: IWS, P.O. Box 1530, Santa Monica, CA 90406-1530

And you can visit our website at: http://www.integralwaysociety.org

YO SAN UNIVERSITY OF TRADITIONAL CHINESE MEDICINE

"Not just a medical career, but a lifetime commitment to raising one's spiritual standard."

In response to the growing interest in Taoism and natural health care in the West, in January 1989 we formed Yo San University of Traditional Chinese Medicine, a nonprofit educational institution under the direction of founder Hua-Ching Ni. Yo San University is the continuation of 38 generations of Ni family practitioners who have handed down the knowledge and wisdom of ancient Chinese healing from father to son.

The foundation of Traditional Chinese Medicine is the spiritual capability to know life, to diagnose a person's problem, and to know how to cure it. We teach students how to care for themselves and others, emphasizing the integration of traditional knowledge and modern science, but the true application of Traditional Chinese Medicine is the practical application of one's own spiritual development.

The purpose of Yo San University is to train practitioners of the highest caliber in Traditional Chinese Medicine, which includes acupuncture, herbology, and spiritual development. We offer a complete Master's degree program which is approved by the California State Department of Education and which meets all requirements for state licensure.

We invite you to inquire into our program for a creative and rewarding career as a holistic physician. Classes are also open to persons interested in self-enrichment. For more information, please fill out the form below or visit our website at: http://www.yosan.edu.

Yo San University of Traditional Chinese Medicine
13315 W. Washington Boulevard, Suite 200
Los Angeles, CA 90066
Phone: (310) 577-3000   Fax: (310) 577-3033

❑ Please send me information on the Masters degree program in
Traditional Chinese Medicine.

❑ Please send me information on health workshops and seminars.

❑ Please send me information on continuing education for acupuncturists and
health professionals.

Name: _____

Address: _____

City: _____ State: _____ Zip: _____

Phone: (daytime) _____ (evening) _____

MOVEMENT TRAINING & TEACHER CERTIFICATION

Chi Gong (also known as *qigong* or *chi kung*) is "energy work" and involves various methods of developing the *chi* or life energy of the body as the foundation of a healthy and happy life. The Ni Family Chi Movements Arts encompass a variety of Chi Gong forms that incorporate specific methods of breathing, meditative focus, physical movement, and energy guidance. The major benefits are general strengthening, enhanced flexibility and tone, relaxation and stress reduction, increased mental clarity, and the balancing of mind, body, and spirit leading to overall improved health, well-being, and increased longevity. These movement arts are an excellent complement to a healthy lifestyle.

The Ni family has gathered, developed, and passed down these useful Chi Gong forms through many generations, continuing their family's ancient spiritual tradition of Esoteric Taoism from the time of the Yellow Emperor and before. The Ni Family Chi Movement Arts include varieties of T'ai Chi, Eight Treasures, Dao-In, and many health and meditative practices. Please refer to *Strength from Movement: Mastering Chi* by Hua-Ching Ni for an excellent introduction.

The Ni family established the **Chi Health Institute** to promote the wider availability and more effective practice of useful forms of Chi Gong for personal and social improvement. The Institute serves as a custodian of the Ni Family Chi Movement Arts tradition, and actively works to sponsor training opportunities to develop additional training materials and to certify teachers.

We would be happy to assist you in selecting and learning a suitable form. We can provide a directory of certified teachers, information about available training workshops, ongoing classes, and self-study and distance learning options, as well as information about a variety of instructional materials. We would also be happy to assist you in becoming a certified teacher of the Ni Family Chi Movement Arts.

Please write to us at the address below for more information, and include your name, e-mail, telephone number, mailing address, and any special interests, or visit our website at www.chihealth.org. We look forward to helping you further your growth.

Chi Health Institute
P.O. Box 2035
Santa Monica, CA 90406
http://www.chihealth.org

HERBS USED BY ANCIENT MASTERS

The pursuit of health is an innate human desire. Long ago, Chinese esoteric Taoists went to the high mountains to contemplate nature, strengthen their bodies, empower their minds, and develop their spirit. From their studies and cultivation, they developed Chinese alchemy and chemistry, herbology, acupuncture, the *I Ching*, astrology, T'ai Chi Ch'uan, Chi Gong, and many other useful tools for health and self-improvement.

The ancient Taoists also passed down methods for attaining longevity and spiritual immortality, one of which was the development of herbal formulas that could be used to increase one's energy and heighten vitality. The Ni family has preserved this treasured collection of herbal formulas for centuries.

Now, through Traditions of Tao, the Ni family makes these ancient formulas available to assist you in building a strong foundation for health and spiritual self-cultivation. For further information about Traditions of Tao herbal products, please complete the following form or visit our website at: http://www.traditionsoftao.com or http://www.taoofwellness.com.

Traditions of Tao
13315 W. Washington Boulevard, Suite 200
Los Angeles, CA 90066
Phone: (310) 302-1206   Fax: (310) 302-1208

❑ Please send me a Traditions of Tao catalog.

Name: _____

Address: _____

City: _____ State: _____ Zip: _____

Phone: (daytime) _____ (evening) _____